Knock at a Star

A Child's Introduction to Poetry

Revised Edition

Knock at a Star

A Child's Introduction to Poetry

Revised Edition

X. J. Kennedy
and Dorothy M. Kennedy

Illustrated by
Karen Lee Baker

Little, Brown and Company
Boston   New York   London

ALSO BY THE KENNEDYS:

Talking Like the Rain

First Edition

Original edition published by Little, Brown and Company © 1982

Copyright acknowledgments appear on page 176.

Library of Congress Cataloging-in-Publication Data

Knock at a star : a child's introduction to poetry / [compiled] by X. J. Kennedy
   and Dorothy Kennedy ; illustrated by Karen Lee Baker. — Rev. ed.
       p.   cm.
   Includes index.
   Summary: A collection of poems arranged in such categories as poems that
make you smile, send messages, or share feelings; poems that contain "beats
that repeat" or "word play"; and special kinds of poems such as limericks,
songs, and haiku.
       ISBN 0-316-48436-9 (hc)
       ISBN 0-316-48800-3 (pb)
       1. Children's poetry, American.   2. Children's poetry, English. [1. American
poetry — Collection.   2. English poetry — Collections.]   I. Kennedy, X. J.
II. Kennedy, Dorothy M. (Dorothy Mintzlaff)   III. Baker, Karen Lee, ill.
PS586.3.K58   1999
811.008'09282 — dc21   98-21572

HC: 10 9 8 7 6 5 4 3 2 1
PB: 10 9 8 7 6 5 4 3 2 1

MV-NY

Printed in the United States of America

CONTENTS

Share Feelings 28

Help You Understand People 40

Start You Wondering 51

2 * WHAT'S INSIDE A POEM? 59

Images 61

Word Music 71

Finders-Keepers Poems   139

Haiku   143

4 * DO IT YOURSELF   147

Writing Your Own Poems   149

Ideas   151

1 * WHAT DO POEMS DO?

Make You Smile

Tell Stories

Send Messages

Share Feelings

Help You Understand People

Start You Wondering

MAKE YOU SMILE

Poets, when they write nonsense, can turn our everyday world inside out and stand it on its ear.

Some poems are just for fun.

For instance . . .

Crunchy

With all that morning fiber
And breakfast bran to greet me
I keep away from horses
In case they want to eat me!

Max Fatchen

Commas

Do commas have mommas
Who teach them to pause,
Who comfort and calm them,
And clean their sharp claws?
Who tell them short stories
Of uncommon commas
And send them to bed
In their comma pajamas?

Douglas Florian

My Mother Took Me Skating

My mother took me skating
and we glided on the ice,
I wasn't very good at it
and stumbled more than twice.

My mother made a figure eight,
and since it seemed like fun,
I tried a little trick myself
and made a figure one.

Jack Prelutsky

Learning

I'm learning to say thank you.
And I'm learning to say please.
And I'm learning to use Kleenex,
Not my sweater, when I sneeze.
And I'm learning not to dribble.
And I'm learning not to slurp.
And I'm learning (though it sometimes
    really hurts me)
Not to burp.
And I'm learning to chew softer
When I eat corn on the cob.
And I'm learning that it's much
Much easier to be a slob.

                              Judith Viorst

There Was a Man

There was a man who never was.
This tragedy occurred because
His parents, being none too smart,
Were born two hundred years apart.

Dennis Lee

Algy

Algy met a bear,
The bear met Algy.
The bear was bulgy,
The bulge was Algy.

Anonymous

Who is Anonymous, anyway? Anonymous means "no name." In this book, we give this byline to any poet whose name nobody knows. After Shakespeare, Anonymous may be the second best poet in our language. At least, he and she wrote more good poems than most poets who sign what they write.

The Termite

Some primal termite knocked on wood
And tasted it, and found it good,
And that is why your Cousin May
Fell through the parlor floor today.

Ogden Nash

Spring is sprung

Spring is sprung.
The grass is riz.
I wonder where
The flowers is.

The little bird
Is on the wing—
Aw, that's absurd.

The little wing
Is on the bird.

Anonymous

The Ceiling

Suppose the Ceiling went Outside
And then caught Cold and Up and Died?
The only Thing we'd have for Proof
That he was Gone, would be the Roof;
I think it would be Most Revealing
To find out how the Ceiling's Feeling.

Theodore Roethke

Miss McGillicuddy

When our old baby-sitter quit,
Another sitter came to sit.
She told us as she did the split,
  "I am not a fuddy-duddy.
  I am Miss McGillicuddy."

While she touched her toes, she said,
"Homework should be done in bed.
Rest is best to clear your head.
  First you snooze and then you study."
  So said Miss McGillicuddy.

When it rains, she doesn't fret;
That's because she likes to get
Dripping, dropping, sopping wet.
  "I don't mind if I am muddy."
  Silly Miss McGillicuddy!

Mary Ann Hoberman

Knitted Things

There was a witch who knitted things:
Elephants and playground swings.
She knitted rain,
She knitted night,
But nothing really came out right.
The elephants had just one tusk
And night looked more
Like dawn or dusk.
The rain was snow
And when she tried
To knit an egg
It came out fried.
She knitted birds
With buttonholes
And twenty rubber butter rolls.
She knitted blue angora trees.
She purl stitched countless purple fleas.
She knitted a palace in need of a darn.
She knitted a battle and ran out of yarn.
She drew out a strand
Of her gleaming, green hair
And knitted a lawn
Till she just wasn't there.

Karla Kuskin

Getting Together

Do you prefer
giblets to triplets,
or triplets to giblets,
or not?
Do you like carrots
as dearly as parrots,
or parrots far better,
or what?

Do you prefer
lizards to blizzards,
and blizzards and lizards
to lumps?
Do you like wrinkles
better than crinkles
and crinkles much better
than mumps?

Do you think slippers
are better than flippers,
and flippers are better
than flaps?
Then don't ever bother
to marry another.
We were meant for each other!
Perhaps.

N. M. *Bodecker*

TELL STORIES

When you watch a superhero trashing a monster on TV, you're enjoying a kind of storytelling that began very long ago. The oldest long story in the western half of the world is *The Odyssey*, written in Greek. Its superhero tangles with a one-eyed giant, a witch who turns men into pigs, and other menaces. Nowadays, we think of stories as things found only in books, but in fact, until a few hundred years ago, most stories were poetry and were primarily sung or spoken aloud. People who couldn't read heard their stories from storytellers who would sing or chant or recite from memory.

The Odyssey is not only old, but long: more than fifteen thousand lines. Later, around the thirteenth century in England, short story-songs called ballads became popular. Most are about lovers who die sadly, ghosts who return from the grave, heroes, such as Robin Hood, and other interesting people. Ballads are still being sung, and some have been written in America. Other kinds of story-poems are still being written, too. Lately, some have been *very* short, like this:

A peanut sat on a railroad track

A peanut sat on a railroad track,
His heart was all a-flutter.
The five-fifteen came rushing by—
Toot toot! Peanut butter!

Anonymous

Today, as in ancient times, poets like to spin good yarns. And still, some of the best poets tell of magic and marvels.

The Knowledgeable Child

I always see,—I don't know why,—
If any person's going to die.

That's why nobody talks to me.
There was a man who came to tea,

And when I saw that he would die
I went to him and said "Good-bye,

"I shall not see you any more."
He died that evening. Then, next door,

They had a little girl: she died
Nearly as quick, and Mummy cried

And cried; and ever since that day
She's made me promise not to say.

But folks are still afraid of me,
And, where they've children, nobody

Will let me next or nigh to them
For fear I'll say good-bye to them.

L. A. G. *Strong*

The Purist

I give you now Professor Twist,
A conscientious scientist.
Trustees exclaimed, "He never bungles!"
And sent him off to distant jungles.
Camped on a tropic riverside,
One day he missed his loving bride.
She had, the guide informed him later,
Been eaten by an alligator.
Professor Twist could not but smile.
"You mean," he said, "a crocodile."

Ogden Nash

What Has Happened to Lulu?

What has happened to Lulu, mother?
    What has happened to Lu?
There's nothing in her bed but an old rag doll
    And by its side a shoe.

Why is her window wide, mother,
    The curtain flapping free,
And only a circle on the dusty shelf
    Where her money-box used to be?

Why do you turn your head, mother,
    And why do the tear-drops fall?
And why do you crumple that note on the fire
    And say it is nothing at all?

I woke to voices late last night,
    I heard an engine roar.
Why do you tell me the things I heard
    Were a dream and nothing more?

I heard somebody cry, mother,
In anger or in pain,
But now I ask you why, mother,
You say it was a gust of rain.

Why do you wander about as though
You don't know what to do?
What has happened to Lulu, mother?
What has happened to Lu?

Charles Causley

You'll notice that in "What Has Happened to Lulu?" and other poems in the book so far, the lines end in sounds that chime together—Lu / shoe, free / be, and so on. A poem that does this is said to rhyme. We go into this matter further in the "Word Music" section of this book. Meanwhile, please remember that only *some* poems rhyme. They don't always need to. Here's one that doesn't:

Coyote Blue

Coyote had a bad case
of the blues one day.
His paws deep in his pockets,
he padded about
pretending that he was invisible.

Lone-Hare, in passing with great haste,
accidentally bumped into Coyote,
who, very upset and shaken,
snapped at Lone-Hare, "How dare you
bump into me. Can't you see
that I'm invisible!"

Judith Mountain-Leaf Volborth

But Only the Breeze . . .

I found the robin lying still
beside the shed.
Its orange side was down,
its wings half spread.

I wanted it to flutter, rise
up to the sky;
I begged it to try . . .

But only the breeze
that lifted a wing,
only the breeze,
did anything.

Constance Levy

The Outlaw

Into the house of a Mrs. MacGruder
Came a very big outlaw
With a real six-shooter,
And he kicked the door
With his cowboy boot
And he searched the place
For valuable loot,
And he didn't take off his cowboy hat
But he quickly unlimbered his cowboy gat
And he cocked the gun
And he took his aim
And he called that Mrs. MacG by name
And he said in a terrible outlaw drawl,
"Git me that cake . . . and git it all!"

And Mrs. MacGruder patted his head,
"You may have a slice with some milk," she said.

Felice Holman

A Story That Could Be True

If you were exchanged in the cradle and
your real mother died
without ever telling the story
then no one knows your name,
and somewhere in the world
your father is lost and needs you
but you are far away.

He can never find
how true you are, how ready.
When the great wind comes
and the robberies of the rain
you stand on the corner shivering.
The people who go by—
you wonder at their calm.

They miss the whisper that runs
any day in your mind,
"Who are you really, wanderer?"—
and the answer you have to give
no matter how dark and cold
the world around you is:
"Maybe I'm a king."

William Stafford

Mummy Slept Late and Daddy Fixed Breakfast

Daddy fixed the breakfast.
He made us each a waffle.
It looked like gravel pudding.
It tasted something awful.

"Ha, ha," he said, "I'll try again.
This time I'll get it right."
But what I got was in between
Bituminous and anthracite.

"A little too well done? Oh well,
I'll have to start all over."
That time what landed on my plate
Looked like a manhole cover.

I tried to cut it with a fork:
The fork gave off a spark.
I tried a knife and twisted it
Into a question mark.

I tried it with a hack-saw.
I tried it with a torch.
It didn't even make a dent.
It didn't even scorch.

The next time Dad gets breakfast
When Mommy's sleeping late,
I think I'll skip the waffles.
I'd sooner eat the plate!

John Ciardi

Can a man work faster than a powerful machine? Such a man is remembered in a famous storytelling song. No, not Superman. John Henry.

Scholars believe John Henry really lived, although the song draws him larger than life. A black workingman, he helped to build a railroad tunnel a mile and a quarter long. It went through a mountain near Hinton, West Virginia.

John Henry was a steel-driver, no doubt the greatest the Chesapeake and Ohio Railroad ever had. A steel-driver was the man who hammered a drill into a sheet of rock, making a hole to plant explosives in. His helper, the "shaker," held the drill, giving it a twist by hand after each blow of the steel-driver's hammer. That was hard, backbreaking work, and when a machine was invented to do the job, John Henry's captain, or boss tunnel-builder, wanted to give it a try. So he set John Henry and the steam drill to work side by side, racing each other.

How the contest turned out has been sung, in different versions, for more than a hundred years.

John Henry

When John Henry was a little tiny baby
Sitting on his mama's knee,
He picked up a hammer and a little piece of steel
Saying, "Hammer's going to be the death of me, Lord, Lord,
    Hammer's going to be the death of me."

John Henry was a man just six feet high,
Nearly two feet and a half across his breast.
He'd hammer with a nine-pound hammer all day
And never get tired and want to rest, Lord, Lord,
    And never get tired and want to rest.

John Henry went up on the mountain
And he looked one eye straight up its side.
The mountain was so tall and John Henry was so small,
He laid down his hammer and he cried, "Lord, Lord,"
   He laid down his hammer and he cried.

John Henry said to his captain,
"Captain, you go to town,
  Bring me back a TWELVE-pound hammer, please,
And I'll beat that steam drill down, Lord, Lord,
   I'll beat that steam drill down."

The captain said to John Henry,
"I believe this mountain's sinking in."
  But John Henry said, "Captain, just you stand aside—
It's nothing but my hammer catching wind, Lord, Lord,
   It's nothing but my hammer catching wind."

John Henry said to his shaker,
"Shaker, boy, you better start to pray,
  'Cause if my TWELVE-pound hammer miss that little piece of
    steel,
Tomorrow'll be your burying day, Lord, Lord,
   Tomorrow'll be your burying day."

John Henry said to his captain,
"A man is nothing but a man,
  But before I let your steam drill beat me down,
I'd die with this hammer in my hand, Lord, Lord,
   I'd die with this hammer in my hand."

The man that invented the steam drill,
He figured he was mighty high and fine,
  But John Henry sunk the steel down fourteen feet
While the steam drill only made nine, Lord, Lord,
   The steam drill only made nine.

John Henry hammered on the right-hand side.
Steam drill kept driving on the left.
John Henry beat that steam drill down.
But he hammered his poor heart to death, Lord, Lord.
    He hammered his poor heart to death.

Well, they carried John Henry down the tunnel
And they laid his body in the sand.
Now every woman riding on a C and O train
Says, "There lies my steel-driving man, Lord, Lord
    There lies my steel-driving man."

Anonymous

SEND MESSAGES

Poems often have a point to make. They leave us something to think about, and they don't waste words.

Before Starting

A burro once, sent by express,
His shipping ticket on his bridle,
Ate up his name and his address,
And in some warehouse, standing idle,
He waited till he like to died.
The moral hardly needs the showing:
Don't keep things locked up deep inside—
Say who you are and where you're going.

Walker Gibson

Smokescreen

My CD-ROM just turned me on
With graphics of high tech;
This information highway's great—
If I don't have a wreck.

Charles Ghigna

Subway Rush Hour

Mingled
breath and smell
so close
mingled
black and white
so near
no room for fear.

Langston Hughes

This next poem was first printed in 1917, before laws prevented children from working in factories.

The Golf Links

The golf links lie so near the mill
   That almost every day
The laboring children can look out
   And see the men at play.

Sarah N. Cleghorn

Spectacular

Listen,
a bird is singing.
Look,
up there!
He's on the rooftop
clinging
to the TV aerial,
singing
on prime time—
and no sponsor!

Lilian Moore

Childhood

I used to think that grown-up people chose
To have stiff backs and wrinkles round their nose,
And veins like small fat snakes on either hand,
On purpose to be grand.
Till through the banisters I watched one day
My great-aunt Etty's friend who was going away,
And how her onyx beads had come unstrung.
I saw her grope to find them as they rolled;
And then I knew that she was helplessly old,
As I was helplessly young.

Frances Cornford

Poor

I heard of poor.
It means hungry, no food,
No shoes, no place to live.
Nothing good.

It means winter nights
And being cold.
It is lonely, alone,
Feeling old.

Poor is a tired face.
Poor is thin.
Poor is standing outside
Looking in.

Myra Cohn Livingston

Raccoon

The raccoon wears a black mask,
And he washes everything
Before he eats it. If you
Give him a cube of sugar,
He'll wash it away and weep.
Some of life's sweetest pleasures
Can be enjoyed only if
You don't mind a little dirt.
Here a false face won't help you.

Kenneth Rexroth

Landscape

What will you find at the edge of the world?
A footprint,
a feather,
desert sand swirled?
A tree of ice,
a rain of stars,
or a junkyard of cars?

What will there be at the rim of the earth?
A mollusc,
a mammal,
a new creature's birth?
Eternal sunrise,
immortal sleep,
or cars piled up in a rusty heap?

Eve Merriam

A word is dead

A word is dead
When it is said,
Some say.
I say it just
Begins to live
That day.

Emily Dickinson

Oh, God of dust and rainbows

Oh, God of dust and rainbows, help us see
That without dust the rainbow would not be.

Langston Hughes

Time to Plant Trees

Time to plant trees is when you're young
So you will have them to walk among—

So, aging, you can walk in shade
That you and time together made.

James Hayford

SHARE FEELINGS

How do you feel when you see a rainbow after a storm? Are you surprised? Happy? Relieved that the storm is over? William Wordsworth begins a poem by telling us how *he* feels:

> My heart leaps up when I behold
> A rainbow in the sky.

Maybe the poet says what you feel about rainbows but haven't been able to say. Or maybe rainbows don't usually make you feel anything special at all. By sharing with you his wonder and joy, the poet invites you—when next you see a rainbow—to feel a special way about it, too.

Short poems that share feelings are called lyrics. The word *lyric*, by the way, comes from *lyre*—a stringed instrument that in ancient Greece made music to go with words, either sung or spoken. (That's why the words to songs are also called lyrics today.)

Poetry can express many different moods: happiness, sadness, anger, fear, loneliness. What feelings do you find in these lyric poems?

Christmas morning i

Christmas morning i
got up before the others and
ran
naked across the plank
floor into the front
room to see grandmama
sewing a new
button on my last year
ragdoll.

Carol Freeman

And Stands There Sighing

Down from the north on the north wind flying
the wild geese come: I hear their crying.
Run to the door, and do not mind
that when they are gone, you'll be left behind.
For whoever hears the great flocks crying
longs to be off, and stands there, sighing.

Elizabeth Coatsworth

My Brother

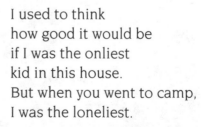

I used to think
how good it would be
if I was the onliest
kid in this house.
But when you went to camp,
I was the loneliest.

Bobbi Katz

Leave Me Alone

Loving care!
Too much to bear.
Leave me alone!

Don't brush my hair,
Don't pat my head,
Don't tuck me in
Tonight in bed,
Don't ask me if I want a sweet,
Don't fix my favorite things to eat,
Don't give me lots of good advice,
And most of all just don't be nice.

But when I've wallowed well in sorrow,
Be nice to me again tomorrow.

Felice Holman

Look Out!

The witches mumble horrid chants,
You're scolded by five thousand aunts,
  A Martian pulls a fearsome face
  And hurls you into Outer Space,
You're tied in front of whistling trains,
A tomahawk has sliced your brains,
  The tigers snarl, the giants roar,
  You're sat on by a dinosaur.
In vain you're shouting "Help" and "Stop,"
The walls are spinning like a top,
  The earth is melting in the sun
  And all the horror's just begun.
And, oh, the screams, the thumping hearts
That awful night before school starts.

Max Fatchen

Zimmer in Grade School

In grade school I wondered
Why I had been born
To wrestle in the ashy puddles,
With my square nose
Streaming mucus and blood,
My knuckles puffed from combat
And the old nun's ruler.
I feared everything: God,
Learning, and my schoolmates.
I could not count, spell, or read.
My report card proclaimed
These scarlet failures.
My parents wrang their loving hands.
My guardian angel wept constantly.

But I could never hide anything.
If I peed my pants in class
The puddle was always quickly evident,
My worst mistakes were at
The blackboard for Jesus and all
The saints to see.
                 Even now
When I hide behind elaborate masks
It is always known that I am Zimmer,
The one who does the messy papers
And fractures all his crayons,
Who spits upon the radiators
And sits all day in shame
Outside the office of the principal.

Paul Zimmer

Losing Face

Finally Mother is proud
of something
I have done.
"My girl won
the art contest,"
she tells the world,
smiling so big
and laughing so loud
her gold tooth
shows.

I'm the only one
who knows
how I drew so well,
erasing the perfect lines
I traced,
drawing worse ones
on purpose
in their place.
I feel awful.
I want to tell.

But I don't want to lose
Mother's glowing
proud face.

Janet S. Wong

The 1st

What I remember about that day
is boxes stacked across the walk
and couch springs curling through the air
and drawers and tables balanced on the curb
and us, hollering,
leaping up and around
happy to have a playground;

nothing about the emptied rooms
nothing about the emptied family

Lucille Clifton

Listening to grownups quarreling,

standing in the hall against the
wall with my little brother, blown
like leaves against the wall by their
voices, my head like a pingpong ball
between the paddles of their anger:
I knew what it meant
to tremble like a leaf.

Cold with their wrath, I heard
the claws of the rain
pounce. Floods
poured through the city,
skies clapped over me,
and I was shaken, shaken
like a mouse
between their jaws.

Ruth Whitman

Hide and Seek

The trees are tall, but the moon small,
My legs feel rather weak,
For Avis, Mavis and Tom Clarke
Are hiding somewhere in the dark
And it's my turn to seek.

Suppose they lay a trap and play
A trick to frighten me?
Suppose they plan to disappear
And leave me here, half-dead with fear,
Groping from tree to tree?

Alone, alone, all on my own
And then perhaps to find
Not Avis, Mavis and young Tom
But monsters to run shrieking from,
Mad monsters of no kind?

Robert Graves

The Hurt Doe

Four deer walk by my front yard this evening.
One of the two does lingers behind
with a hurt leg. What can I do?
"Let it go; let it go,"
the grown-ups say.
"It's the way of things."
But I worry.
What will happen to it?
Why can't I help?

Emanuel diPasquale

An Historic Moment

The man said,
 after inventing poetry,
"WOW!"
 and did a full somersault.

William J. Harris

Country School

The Apple Valley School has closed its books,
wiped off its blackboard, put away its chalk;
the valley children with their parents' looks
ride buses down the road their parents walked.

The Apple Valley School is full of bales,
and the bell was auctioned off a year ago.
Under the teeter-totter, spotted quail
have nested where the grass would never grow.

The well is dry where boys caught garter snakes
and chased the girls into their memories.
High on the hill, nobody climbs to shake
the few ripe apples from the broken tree.

While I Slept

While I slept, while I slept and the night grew colder
She would come to my room, stepping softly
And draw a blanket about my shoulder
While I slept.

While I slept, while I slept in the dark, still heat
She would come to my bedside, stepping coolly
And smooth the twisted, troubled sheet
While I slept.

Now she sleeps, sleeps under quiet rain
While nights grow warm or nights grow colder.
And I wake, and sleep, and wake again
While she sleeps.

Robert Francis

HELP YOU UNDERSTAND PEOPLE

What makes Jimmy keep to himself and avoid the other kids? Why does Robin's grandfather spend so much time looking out the window? How does it feel to be homeless? Often we wonder about people who cross our paths every day. Sometimes we find answers just by watching and listening, sometimes by asking people to share their thoughts and feelings. Poems, too, can give us insight into why people act as they do. Even a small poem, by showing us in words what a person looks like or what he or she is thinking, can help us understand more about our families, our friends, and the other people on our planet.

People

Some people talk and talk
and never say a thing.
Some people look at you
and birds begin to sing.

Some people laugh and laugh
and yet you want to cry.
Some people touch your hand
and music fills the sky.

Charlotte Zolotow

Puerto Ricans in New York

She enters the bus demurely
with the delicate dark face
the Spaniards first saw
on an island in the Caribbean
and he follows—
a tall gentle lad.
He smiles pleasantly, shyly,
at her now and then,
but she does not look at him,
looking away demurely.
She holds a small package in her hand—
perhaps a nightgown—
and he a larger package:
a brand-new windowshade.

Charles Reznikoff

Narcissa

Some of the girls are playing jacks.
Some are playing ball.
But small Narcissa is not playing
Anything at all.

Small Narcissa sits upon
A brick in her back yard
And looks at tiger-lilies,
And shakes her pigtails hard.

First she is an ancient queen
In pomp and purple veil.
Soon she is a singing wind.
And, next, a nightingale.

How fine to be Narcissa,
A-changing like all that!
While sitting still, as still, as still
As anyone ever sat!

Gwendolyn Brooks

The Knowing One

Life will hand Mary
No harder task
Than to know the right answer
And have no one ask.

Jean Little

The Park People

A real old man
and a real old lady
stay out in the park.
They go into a little house
to sleep when it gets dark.
They burn newspapers
to keep them warm
They wrap themselves in rags
and when it rains
they cover their heads
with old brown paper bags.

I am very sorry
that they have no place to stay
'cause they're real old
and very nice
and shouldn't live that way.

Karama Fufuka

Myrtle

Wearing her yellow rubber slicker,
Myrtle, our *Journal* carrier,
has come early through rain and darkness
to bring us the news.
A woman of thirty or so,
with three small children at home,
she's told me she likes
a long walk by herself in the morning.
And with pride in her work,
she's wrapped the news neatly in plastic—
a bread bag, beaded with rain,
that reads WONDER.
From my doorway I watch her
flicker from porch to porch as she goes,
a yellow candle flame
no wind or weather dare extinguish.

Ted Kooser

Naturally, the people you know earliest, before you know any others, are the ones you live with. Here are a few poems about family members. (Not that everyone's family is alike!)

Two People

She reads the paper,
while he turns on TV;
she likes the mountains,
he craves the sea.

He'd rather drive,
she'll take the plane;
he waits for sunshine,
she walks in the rain.

He gulps down cold drinks,
she sips at hot;
he asks, "Why go?"
She asks, "Why not?"

In just about everything
they disagree,
but they love one another
and they both love me.

Eve Merriam

Mama's Bouquets

Sun every day
Heat year round
Mama sang
As she clipped flowers
In the garden
    Surprising butterflies
    And hummingbirds
Each day

Mama's bouquets
In every room
Sweetened
And brightened the air
Wherever we looked
Flowers
Indoors and out
Always

We are grown and gone
Our rooms are silent
Still
Mama sings
As she gathers flowers
    Surprising butterflies
    And hummingbirds
Each day

We say,
"Save your strength, Ma!"
We ask,
"Who sees bouquets
In empty rooms?"

Mama says,
"God is here
Always
With the flowers
And my song
Each day
When you are gone."

Ashley Bryan

My Mother

My mother
Wasn't like
Some others.

She didn't
Make cakes or
Candied apples.

She sat down
Beside her
Sewing basket

And stayed
Up late
Reading poetry.

Valerie Worth

Dad

Watch out.
Mad, he snaps
like a turtle.
His face blows up
round.
His mouth thins
to a frown.
He sticks his neck out
in a dare.
Beware.
Quick as he strikes,
he draws back,
hiding in his tough
hard shell.

Janet S. Wong

Sundays

For lunch
Dad wore a white shirt
with cuffs stiff
as the ace of spades,
knit pants,
and loafers.

After lunch
we walked to the park
as he rubbed the baseball
with hands as tough and smooth
as the underside of a tortoise.

At the backstop,
as slowly as bread rising,
he rolled up his sleeves
before hitting fly balls
that seemed to skip off the sun
before landing
still warm
in my mitt.

Paul B. Janeczko

grandmother

if i were to see
her shape from a mile away
i'd know so quickly
that it would be her.
the purple scarf
and the plastic
shopping bag.
if i felt
hands on my head
i'd know that those
were her hands
warm and damp
with the smell
of roots.
if i heard
a voice
coming from
a rock
i'd know
and her words
would flow inside me
like the light
of someone
stirring ashes
from a sleeping fire
at night.

Ray A. Young Bear

START YOU WONDERING

Poets, like the rest of us, love magic and mystery. Sometimes they'll tell us of ghosts, werewolves, dragons, creatures from far-off worlds. At other times, they'll weave a different kind of magic. They may show us everyday, ordinary things, but show them in new ways. For instance, did you ever think that an old toy magnet could be wonderful?

Magnet

This small
Flat horseshoe
Is sold for
A toy: we are
Told that it
Will pick up pins
And it does, time
After time; later
It lies about,
Getting its red
Paint chipped, being
Offered pins less
Often, until at
Last we leave it
Alone: then
It leads its own
Life, trading
Secrets with
The North Pole,
Reading
Invisible messages
From the sun.

Valerie Worth

Key Ring

When my grandfather was very old
to one small room confined
he gave me his big bunch of keys to hold.

I asked, "Do they unlock every door there is?
And what would I find inside?"

He answered, "Mysteries and more mysteries.
You can't tell till you've tried."

Then as I swung the heavy ring around
the keys made a chuckling sound.

Virginia Hamilton Adair

The Magical Mouse

I am the magical mouse
I don't eat cheese
I eat sunsets
And the tops of trees
I don't wear fur
I wear funnels
Of lost ships and the weather
That's under dead leaves

I am the magical mouse
I don't fear cats
Or woodsowls
I do as I please
Always
I don't eat crusts
I am the magical mouse
I eat
Little birds—and maidens

That taste like dust

Kenneth Patchen

Daniel Boone
1735–1820

When Daniel Boone goes by, at night,
The phantom deer arise
And all lost, wild America
Is burning in their eyes.

Stephen Vincent Benét

The White Horse

The youth walks up to the white horse, to put its halter on
and the horse looks at him in silence.
They are so silent they are in another world.

D. H. *Lawrence*

The Child on the Shore

Wind, wind, give me back my feather
Sea, sea, give me back my ring
Death, death, give me back my mother
   So that she can hear me sing.

Song, song, go and tell my daughter
Tell her that I wear the ring
Say I fly upon the feather
   Fallen from the falcon's wing.

Ursula K. *LeGuin*

A Boot

O beautiful
was the werewolf
in his evil forest.
We took him
to the carnival
and he started
   crying
when he saw
the Ferris wheel.
Electric
green and red tears
flowed down
his furry cheeks.
He looked
like a boat
out on the dark
water.

Richard Brautigan

Winter Song

I saw two crows upon a tree
 Scrawking and cawing endlessly:
"Light on the leaves, and then goodbye.
 What is the cold wind's alibi?"
      "I do not know," said I.

I saw the snow truck up the street,
 Taking the slush from the curb to eat:
"Think of forsythia, last July—

Where are the petals that filled the sky?"
　"Ask me again," said I.

I saw a sparrow, small and alive,
Skipping for food in the snowy drive:
"Do we endure in God's great eye?
Is there a green that does not die?"
　"We'll wait and see," said I.

Dennis Lee

Green Candles

"There's someone at the door," said gold candlestick:
"Let her in quick, let her in quick!"
"There is a small hand groping at the handle.
　Why don't you turn it?" asked green candle.

"Don't go, don't go," said the Hepplewhite chair,
　"Lest you find a strange lady there."
"Yes, stay where you are," whispered the white wall:
"There is nobody there at all."

"I know her little foot," gray carpet said:
"Who but I should know her light tread?"
"She shall come in," answered the open door,
"And not," said the room, "go out anymore."

Humbert Wolfe

The Old Stone House

Nothing on the grey roof, nothing on the brown,
Only a little greening where the rain drips down;
Nobody at the window, nobody at the door,
Only a little hollow which a foot once wore;
But still I tread on tiptoe, still tiptoe on I go,
Past nettles, porch, and weedy well, for oh, I know
A friendless face is peering, and a clear still eye
Peeps closely through the casement as my step goes by.

Walter de la Mare

2 * WHAT'S INSIDE A POEM?

Images

Word Music

Beats That Repeat

Likenesses

Word Play

IMAGES

Most of us like to bite into a tart, juicy apple. We wrinkle our noses if we smell a fish lying on a beach. We enjoy the music of an orchestra, the sight of a blue jay hopping on the snow, the warmth and fuzziness of a woolly blanket. We take in the world around us through our five senses: sight, hearing, smell, taste, touch.

Most noses respond to the smell of bread baking in the oven. You may know you like that aroma, but can you catch it in words? Poets are willing to try. They can't make you actually *smell* bread baking, but if they are skillful, they come close.

When a poet tries to capture in words how something looks, tastes, smells, feels, or sounds, those descriptions are called images. Images can even help us imagine heat or cold. When John Keats wants us to sense how cold it is on a bitter evening, he writes: "The hare limped trembling through the frozen grass" — a line that almost makes you want to go *brrrr-r-r*!

Good Hot Dogs
FOR KIKI

Fifty cents apiece
To eat our lunch
We'd run
Straight from school
Instead of home
Two blocks
Then the store
That smelled like steam
You ordered
Because you had the money
Two hot dogs and two pops for here
Everything on the hot dogs
Except pickle lily
Dash those hot dogs
Into buns and splash on
All that good stuff
Yellow mustard and onions
And french fries piled on top all
Rolled up in a piece of wax
Paper for us to hold hot
In our hands
Quarters on the counter
Sit down
Good hot dogs
We'd eat
Fast till there was nothing left
But salt and poppy seeds even
The little burnt tips
Of french fries
We'd eat
You humming
And me swinging my legs

Sandra Cisneros

My Fingers

My fingers are antennae.
Whatever they touch:
Bud, rose, apple,
Cellophane, crutch —
They race the feel
Into my brain,
Plant it there and
Begin again.
This is how I knew
Hot from cold
Before I was even
Two years old.
This is how I can tell,
Though years away,
That elephant hide
Feels leathery grey.
My brain never loses
A touch I bring:
Frail of an eggshell,
Pull of a string,
Beat of a pulse
That tells me life
Thumps in a person
But not in a knife.
Signs that say:
"Please do not touch,"
Disappoint me
Very much.

Mary O'Neill

September

The breezes taste
   Of apple peel.
The air is full
   Of smells to feel—

Ripe fruit, old footballs,
   Burning brush,
New books, erasers,
   Chalk, and such.

The bee, his hive
   Well-honeyed, hums,
And Mother cuts
   Chrysanthemums.

Like plates washed clean
   With suds, the days
Are polished with
   A morning haze.

John Updike

Bull snake   rattle

Bull snake   rattle
snake
cottonmouth
sliding through grass
whipping
your way along the water

Show me how you
loop your scales
how you slide your
S-curves
scribbling no word
and   with a hiss
dis-
appearing!

Barbara Juster Esbensen

Surprise

I lift the toilet seat
as if it were the nest of a bird
and I see cat tracks
all around the edge of the bowl.

Richard Brautigan

66

Waiting for the Storm

Breeze sent a wrinkling darkness
Across the bay. I knelt
Beneath an upturned boat,
And, moment by moment, felt

The sand at my feet grow colder,
The damp air chill and spread.
Then the first raindrops sounded
On the hull above my head.

Timothy Steele

Snowy Benches

Do parks get lonely
in winter, perhaps,
when benches have only
snow on their laps?

Aileen Fisher

Peach

Touch it to your cheek and it's soft
as a velvet newborn mouse
who has to strive
to be alive.

Bite in. Runny
honey
blooms on your tongue—
as if you've bitten open
a whole hive.

Rose Rauter

Spruce Woods

It's so still
today that a
dipping bough means
a squirrel
has gone through

A. R. *Ammons*

The Runner

On a flat road runs the well-trained runner,
He is lean and sinewy with muscular legs,
He is thinly clothed, he leans forward as he runs,
With lightly closed fists and arms partially raised.

Walt Whitman

This Is a Night

This is a night on which to pity cats
hunting through dripping hedgerows,
making wet way
through grasses heavy with rain,
their delicate stepping
tense with distaste,
their soft and supple coats
sodden, for all their care.
This is a night
to pity cats which have no house to go to,
no stove, no saucer of milk, no lowered hand
sleeking a head, no voice to say, "Poor kitty."
This is a night
on which to weep for outcasts, for all those
who know the rain but do not know the shelter.

Elizabeth Coatsworth

Earthy Anecdote

Every time the bucks went clattering
Over Oklahoma
A firecat bristled in the way.

Wherever they went,
They went clattering,
Until they swerved
In a swift, circular line
To the right,
Because of the firecat.

Or until they swerved
In a swift, circular line
To the left,
Because of the firecat.

The bucks clattered.
The firecat went leaping,
To the right, to the left,
And
Bristled in the way.

Later, the firecat closed his bright eyes
And slept.

Wallace Stevens

WORD MUSIC

You or I, standing on a sandy beach in winter, might observe, "The ocean is rough today." A poet, seeing the same waves, might say, as John Updike did in "Winter Ocean":

> Many-maned scud-thumper, tub
> of male whales, maker of worn wood, shrub-
> ruster, sky-mocker, rave!
> portly pusher of waves, wind-slave.

Such a poem is full of word music, as you'll hear if you read it aloud. Good poets choose words with care. They are as much interested in the sound of a word as in its meaning.

In one poem Emily Dickinson calls bees "buccaneers of buzz." The description is an apt one because like pirates (buccaneers), bees roam around and steal something: juice from flowers. Also, the "buzz" imitates their sound.

Edgar Allan Poe uses sounds in much the same way when he talks about "the silken, sad, uncertain rustling of each purple curtain." All those sssssss sounds almost set up a rustling in our ears.

Some poems don't *imitate* sounds, but *repeat* sounds. In Poe's lines, for instance, you can hear *s* sounds repeated, and also *r* sounds repeated inside the words. It's easy to notice such repetition when it comes at the beginnings of words: "Peter Piper picked a peck of pickled peppers." This famous tongue twister repeats the *p* not to sound like a pickle but just because such repetition is fun. We find similar repetition (called alliteration) in familiar sayings: "green as grass," "dead as a doornail," "tried and true." Such sounds often make your lips and mouth work.

In fact, reading good poems out loud, as it's fun to do, you may find that the poems are pretty "chewy." Then you may share what the poet James Wright discovered about reading great poetry in his one-line poem, "Saying Dante Aloud": "You can feel the muscles and veins rippling in widening and rising circles, like a bird in flight under your tongue."

Flittermice

On leathery wings, the flittermice fly
   across the starry August sky.
I watch from my porch as they wheel by.

They rush in a stream through the hay-mow door
   of the old red barn near the sycamore,
to skim the pines and loop and soar.

Like little witches, they dodge and soar,
   then circle the sycamore tree once more.
Four swerve back, through the wide barn door.

I watch the flittermice glide and swing
   across the sky in their magic ring
and wonder how anything

wild as that
could ever be called by the plain name: "Bat."

Patricia Hubbell

The Skaters

Black swallows swooping or gliding
In a flurry of entangled loops and curves,
The skaters skim over the frozen river.
And the grinding click of their skates as they impinge
         upon the surface,
Is like the brushing together of thin wing-tips of
         silver.

John Gould Fletcher

Rain

Like a drummer's brush,
the rain hushes the surfaces of tin porches.

Emanuel diPasquale

Some poets, and most songwriters, love to rhyme. Words rhyme when they end in the same sounds: *spoon* and *baboon*, *murky* and *turkey*. Rhyming words help knit a poem together. Besides, they're interesting to hear. Sometimes, they playfully bring together things you wouldn't expect to find in the same company:

> Julius Caesar,
> That Roman geezer,
> Squashed his wife with a lemon-squeezer.

To rhyme long words that way — words of two or more syllables — is a favorite practice in comic verse.

Some rhymes are exact; other rhymes are looser. Here's the beginning of a poem by Josephine Miles that first gives us an exact rhyme, then an inexact one:

> Went into a shoestore to buy a pair of shoes,
> There was a shoe salesman humming the blues
> Under his breath; over his breath
> Floated a peppermint lifesaver, a little wreath.

As you can see from those last two lines, rhymes depend not on spelling, but on sound. *Breath* and *wreath* are different sounds, though they end in the same letters. A rhyme like that is called an off-rhyme, or a slant rhyme.

Poems don't have to rhyme. In fact, most poems written today don't rhyme at all. Rhyme is just one of the pleasures that poets, if they want to, can provide.

The pickety fence

The pickety fence
The pickety fence
Give it a lick it's
The pickety fence
Give it a lick it's
A clickety fence
Give it a lick it's
A lickety fence
Give it a lick
Give it a lick
Give it a lick
With a rickety stick
Pickety
Pickety
Pickety
Pick

David McCord

Mice Are Nice

Mice
are nice,
and sprigs
of spice,
and jelly beans
and jingles.
Kids
are nice,
but twins
are twice
as nice, they say,
as singles.

N. M. *Bodecker*

My Old Cat

My old cat is dead,
Who would butt me with his head.
He had the sleekest fur.
He had the blackest purr.
Always gentle with us
Was this black puss,
But when I found him today
Stiff and cold where he lay
His look was a lion's,
Full of rage, defiance:
Oh, he would not pretend
That what came was a friend
But met it in pure hate.
Well died, my old cat.

Hal Summers

Stories

Circling by the fire,
My dog, my rough champion,
Coaxes winter out of her fur.
She hears old stories
Leaping in the flames:
The hissing names of cars,
Neighbors' dogs snapping
Like these gone logs,
The cracking of ice . . .
Once, romping through the park,
We dared the creaking pond.
It took the dare and half
Of me into the dark below.
She never let go.

We watch orange tongues
Wagging in the fire
Hush to blue whispers.
Her tail buffs my shoe.
She has one winter left,
Maybe two.

                    J. Patrick Lewis

Analysis of Baseball

It's about
the ball,
the bat,
and the mitt.
Ball hits
bat, or it
hits mitt.
Bat doesn't
hit ball, bat
meets it.
Ball bounces
off bat, flies
air, or thuds
ground (dud)
or it
fits mitt.

Bat waits
for ball
to mate.
Ball hates
to take bat's
bait. Ball
flirts, bat's
late, don't
keep the date.
Ball goes in
(thwack) to mitt,
and goes out
(thwack) back
to mitt.

Ball fits
mitt, but
not all
the time.
Sometimes
ball gets hit
(pow) when bat
meets it,
and sails
to a place
where mitt
has to quit
in disgrace.
That's about
the bases
loaded,
about 40,000
fans exploded.

It's about
the ball,
the bat,
the mitt,
the bases
and the fans.
It's done
on a diamond,
and for fun.
It's about
home, and it's
about run.

May Swenson

Here's a poem that looks like a solid block of words, but it rhymes all the way through. Read it aloud and see!

Football

The Game was ended, and the noise at last had died away, and now they gathered up the boys where they in pieces lay. And one was hammered in the ground by many a jolt and jar; some fragments never have been found, they flew away so far. They found a stack of tawny hair, some fourteen cubits high; it was the half-back, lying there, where he had crawled to die. They placed the pieces on a door, and from the crimson field, that hero then they gently bore, like soldier on his shield. The surgeon toiled the livelong night above the gory wreck; he got the ribs adjusted right, the wishbone and the neck. He soldered on the ears and toes, and got the spine in place, and fixed a gutta-percha nose upon the mangled face. And then he washed his hands and said: "I'm glad that task is done!" The half-back raised his fractured head, and cried: "I call this fun!"

Walt Mason

BEATS THAT REPEAT

Here comes the parade! Drums tap. Trombones slide. Feet tramp the pavement. Arms steadily shuttle to and fro. "That band," we say, "has *rhythm*."

What's rhythm? It's what you get when something happens regularly, again and again and again. Watch a little kid swinging on a swing and you'll notice a rhythm as the board departs and returns, departs and returns. You can also *feel* a rhythm, if you try the swing yourself.

At the ocean, waves roll in — crash — draw back — roll in again. You *see* their rhythm and *hear* their rhythm. Swim in the surf and you'll *feel* their rhythm, too. Rhythms arise from anything that recurs. You can speak of the rhythm of the seasons, the rhythm of day and night.

Poems, too, have rhythms you can see, hear, and feel. To find this out for yourself, read this next poem silently. ("We" are some teenage tough guys. The Golden Shovel is a poolroom where they hang out.)

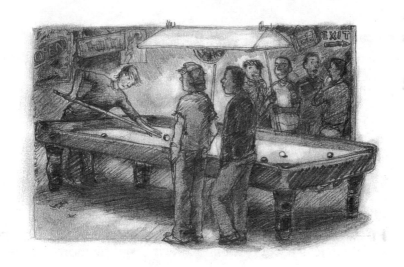

We Real Cool

THE POOL PLAYERS.
SEVEN AT THE GOLDEN SHOVEL.

We real cool. We
Left school. We

Lurk late. We
Strike straight. We

Sing sin. We
Thin gin. We

Jazz June. We
Die soon.

Gwendolyn Brooks

Every sentence in the poem is made of three short words. That gives us a three-beat rhythm: "We real cool. We left school. We lurk late." It's like *wham wham wham. Wham wham wham. Wham wham wham.* Do you notice what else is repeated? Periods. There's a period in the same place in every line. That gives us another rhythm, one made of stops. (Rhythms in poems are made out of little silences, as well as out of *whams*.) Then, the poet gives us still another rhythm in the series of *We*'s. There's one *We* at the end of every line (except the last). So the rhythm of the poem goes like this:

> *wham wham wham* (stop) *wham* (pause)
> *wham wham* (stop) *wham* (pause)
> *wham wham* (stop) *wham* (pause)

And so on.

What we called a *wham*, poets call a stress. A stress is that extra oomph you give a word, or part of a word: a little more loudness or breath. Say *banana*, and you put the stress on the middle syllable (ba-NA-na). Say *tangerine*, and you don't stress the middle syllable; you stress the first syllable and the last (TAN-ger-INE). Every word in "We Real Cool" takes a stress, which makes the rhythm of the poem very powerful. Poets like to arrange words so that the stresses fall into a pattern and so give us a rhythm, as in this nonsense poem:

The Ostrich Is a Silly Bird

The *ostrich is* a *silly bird*
   With *scarcely any mind.*
He *often runs* so *very fast,*
   He *leaves* himself be*hind.*

And *when* he *gets* there, *has* to *stand*
   And *hang* about till *night,*
Without a *blessed thing* to *do*
   Until he *comes* in *sight.*

                  Mary E. Wilkins Freeman

In the poem above, the syllables that you stress are printed in italic letters to help you notice the rhythm. In this poem, the stresses fall on every second syllable, making a rhythm almost as regular as the ticking of a clock.

Poems don't usually stay that regular for very long. If they did, they might grow boring. (Luckily, Freeman's poem is funny — and short.) Here's a poem with a different rhythm in it — a rhythm like the gallop of a horse.

Windy Nights

Whenever the *moon and stars are set,*
   Whenever the *wind* is *high,*
All *night long* in the *dark* and *wet,*
   A *man* goes *riding by.*
Late in the *night* when the *fires* are *out,*
Why does he *gallop* and *gallop* a*bout?*

When*ever* the *trees* are *crying* a*loud,*
   And *ships* are *tossed* at *sea,*
By, on the *highway, low* and *loud,*
   By at the *gallop* goes *he.*
By at the *gallop* he *goes,* and *then*
By he comes *back* at the *gallop* a*gain.*

Robert Louis Stevenson

What suggests hoofbeats? Not just the word *gallop.* It's the rhythm inside the poet's lines. Notice the syllables with no *whams* on them. They tend to come in pairs. That makes for a rocking, or bouncing, rhythm. Read the poem aloud and feel it again. In a good poem, the rhythm—whether regular or changing—goes along with what the poet is saying in it.

Windy Nights

Rumbling in the chimneys,
   Rattling at the doors,
Round the roofs and round the roads
   The rude wind roars;
Raging through the darkness,
   Raving through the trees,
Racing off again across
   The great grey seas.

Rodney Bennett

Windshield Wiper

fog smog   fog smog
tissue paper   tissue paper
clear the blear clear the smear

fog more   fog more
splat splat   downpour
rubber scraper rubber scraper
overshoes   macintosh
bumbershoot   muddle on
slosh through slosh through

drying up   drying up
sky lighter   sky lighter
nearly clear   nearly clear
clearing clearing veer
clear here clear

Eve Merriam

I am Rose

I am Rose my eyes are blue
I am Rose and who are you?
I am Rose and when I sing
I am Rose like anything.

Gertrude Stein

Canis Major

The great Overdog,
That heavenly beast
With a star in one eye,
Gives a leap in the east.

He dances upright
All the way to the west
And never once drops
On his forefeet to rest.

I'm a poor underdog,
But tonight I will bark
With the great Overdog
That romps through the dark.

Robert Frost

Paleface

How pale my back and sides
Compared to horses' hides
Which may be black or bay,
Roan, chestnut, dapple-gray . . .
If polled I would have voted
To be as richly coated.

James Hayford

The opposite of *kite*, I'd say

The opposite of *kite*, I'd say,
Is *yo-yo*. On a breezy day
You take your *kite* and let it *rise*
Upon its string into the skies,
And then you pull it *down* with ease
(Unless it crashes in the trees).
A *yo-yo*, though, drops *down*, and then
You quickly bring it *up* again
By pulling deftly on its string
(If you can work the blasted thing).

Richard Wilbur

My Half

I share a room
with brother Bob.
We share a bunk bed, too.
Half the room belongs to me,
and half to you-know-who.
Of course it's fair to share a room,
but yet I have the feeling
that since I'm on the upper bunk
my half's just on the ceiling.

Florence Parry Heide and
Roxanne Heide Pierce

Blackberry Sweet

Black girl black girl
lips as curved as cherries
full as grape bunches
sweet as blackberries

Black girl black girl
when you walk you are
magic as a rising bird
or a falling star

Black girl black girl
what's your spell to make
the heart in my breast
jump   stop   shake

Dudley Randall

Triolet Against Sisters

Sisters are always drying their hair.
    Locked into rooms, alone,
They pose at the mirror, shoulders bare,
Trying this way and that their hair,
Or fly importunate down the stair
    To answer a telephone.
Sisters are always drying their hair,
    Locked into rooms, alone.

Phyllis McGinley

LIKENESSES

Poets are always putting things together in ways you wouldn't expect. A dog and a thunderstorm don't usually go together. In fact, when thunder and lightning start to boom and flash, all the dogs we know run into the house. But read these lines from a poem:

> Thunder threatens
> Like a sound that rolls around and around
> In a mean dog's throat.

The poet, Martha Sherwood, surprises us. She shows us how a storm and a dog are a lot alike. They make a noise that threatens.

Sometimes poets don't bother with the word *like*; they just go ahead and call one thing another: "Life is just a bowl of cherries," or "Get away from those cookies, you pig!" Nobody thinks a cookie muncher has a tail and oinks. It's just the greedy way he eats that's piglike.

What things are brought together in these poems? What likenesses do the poets reveal?

Fireflies

> An August night —
>   The wind not quite
> A wind, the sky
>   Not just a sky —
> And everywhere
>   The speckled air
> Of summer stars
>   Alive in jars

J. *Patrick Lewis*

Porch Light

At night
the porch light
catches moths
and holds them,
trapped
and
flapping,
in a tight
yellow fist.
Only when I
turn the switch
will it loosen
its hot
grip.

Deborah Chandra

Some common words contain likenesses. . . .

DAISY comes from two Old English words meaning *day's eye*. (As you can hear, *daisy* and *day's eye* still sound almost alike.)

SQUIRREL comes from Greek and means *shadow-tail*.

CIRRUS in Latin means *lock of hair* — so cirrus clouds are the kind that look hairy or fleecy.

Child Frightened by a Thunderstorm

Thunder has nested in the grass all night
and rumpled it, and with its outstretched wings
has crushed the peonies. Its beak was bright,
sharper than garden shears and, clattering,
it snipped bouquets of branches for its bed.
I could not sleep. The thunder's eyes were red.

Ted Kooser

The house-wreckers

The house-wreckers have left the door and a staircase
now leading to the empty room of night.

Charles Reznikoff

Wind and Silver

Greatly shining,
The Autumn moon floats in the thin sky;
And the fish-ponds shake their backs and
    flash their dragon scales
As she passes over them

Amy Lowell

Dreams

Hold fast to dreams
For if dreams die
Life is a broken-winged bird
That cannot fly.

Hold fast to dreams
For when dreams go
Life is a barren field
Frozen with snow.

Langston Hughes

stars

in science today we learned
that stars are a mass of gases that burned
out a long time ago only we don't know
that because we still see the glow

and i remembered my big brother Donny
said he burned out a long time ago and i asked
him did that make him
a star

Nikki Giovanni

**Epigram Engraved on the Collar of a Dog
Which I Gave to His Royal Highness**

I am his Highness' dog at Kew;
Pray tell me, sir, whose dog are you?

Alexander Pope

The Horses of the Sea

The horses of the sea
   Rear a foaming crest,
But the horses of the land
   Serve us best.

The horses of the land
   Munch corn and clover,
While the foaming sea-horses
   Toss and turn over.

Christina Rossetti

The Eagle

He clasps the crag with crookèd hands;
Close to the sun in lonely lands,
Ringed with the azure world, he stands.

The wrinkled sea beneath him crawls;
He watches from his mountain walls,
And like a thunderbolt he falls.

Alfred, Lord Tennyson

Splinter

The voice of the last cricket
across the first frost
is one kind of good-by.
It is so thin a splinter of singing.

Carl Sandburg

Dry Winter

So little snow that the grass in the field
like a terrible thought
has never entirely disappeared. . . .

Jane Kenyon

Spill

the wind scatters
a flock of sparrows—
a handful of small change
spilled suddenly
from the cloud's pocket.

Judith Thurman

The Wind

The wind stood up, and gave a shout;
He whistled on his fingers, and

Kicked the withered leaves about,
And thumped the branches with his hand,

And said he'll kill, and kill, and kill;
And so he will! And so he will!

James Stephens

WORD PLAY

Poets love words—their sounds, their meanings, their rhythms. As we saw in "Word Music," they love words that rhyme and chime and set up echoes with one another. But poets also have discovered the joy of inventing new words. E. E. Cummings, in a poem about spring(on page 103), applies such a new word to the wet earth that little kids dabble in after a rainstorm: *mud-luscious.*

Sometimes poets combine words in fresh ways. They may speed up the word music, turn it up so loud that the poem goes slightly crazy. When they do, they may seem to you more interested in having fun than in making sense, and you may well be right. Sometimes they'll play with two words that sound similar but mean something completely different—that's called a pun. There's a pun in the old joke "How do you get *down* from a duck?" (Answer: "Don't be silly—you can't ride on a duck. You get *down* from a horse!")

In word play, the results can surprise poet and reader. At its best, such word play can be as exciting as a fast game of street hockey, as suspenseful as the next move in a game of chess.

Sing Me a Song of Teapots and Trumpets

Sing me a song
of teapots and trumpets:
Trumpots and teapets
And tippets and taps,
trippers and trappers
and jelly bean wrappers
and pigs in pajamas
with zippers and snaps.

Sing me a song
of sneakers and snoopers:
Snookers and sneapers
and snappers and snacks,
snorkels and snarkles,
a seagull that gargles,
and gargoyles and gryphons
and other knickknacks.

Sing me a song
of parsnips and pickles:
Picsnips and parkles
and pumpkins and pears,
plumbers and mummers
and kettle drum drummers
and plum jam (yum-yum jam)
all over their chairs.

Sing me a song—
but never you mind it!
I've had enough
of this nonsense. Don't cry.
Criers and fliers
and onion ring fryers—
It's more than I want to put up with!
Good-by!

N. M. *Bodecker*

in Just-

in Just-
spring   when the world is mud-
luscious the little
lame balloonman

whistles   far   and wee

and eddieandbill come
running from marbles and
piracies and it's
spring

when the world is puddle-wonderful

the queer
old balloonman whistles
far   and   wee
and bettyandisbel come dancing

from hop-scotch and jump-rope and

it's
spring
and
     the
          goat-footed
balloonMan   whistles
far
and
wee

E. E. *Cummings*

My auntie

My auntie who lives in
Llanfairpwllgwyngyllgogerych-
   wyrndrobwllllantysiliogogogoch
Has asked me to stay.

But unfortunately
Llanfairpwllgwyngyllgogerych-
   wyrndrobwllllantysiliogogogoch
Is a long, long way away.

Will I ever go to
Llanfairpwllgwyngyllgogerych-
   wyrndrobwllllantysiliogogogoch?
It's difficult to say.

Colin West

Plant Life

The dogwood's barking
in the woods.
The horse chestnut
is neighing.
The lady slipper
walks to church.
Jack-in-the-pulpit's
praying.

Alan Benjamin

Song of the Pop-bottlers

Pop bottles pop-bottles
   In pop shops;
The pop-bottles Pop bottles
   Poor Pop drops.

When Pop drops pop-bottles,
   Pop-bottles plop!
Pop-bottle-tops topple!
   Pop mops slop!

Stop! Pop'll drop bottle!
   Stop, Pop, stop!
When Pop bottles pop-bottles,
   Pop-bottles pop!

Morris Bishop

Chess Nut

There's nothing like a game of chess,
   It's patience at its height;
Where else can you just sit and take
   All day to move one knight.

Charles Ghigna

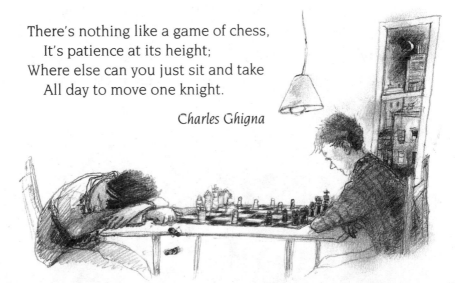

Crickets

they   tell
the   time
of   night
they   tick

the   time
of   night
they   tick
they   tell

of   night
they   tick
and   tell
the   time

they   tick
they   tell
the   time
they   click

Myra Cohn Livingston

Did you eever, iver, over?

Did you eever, iver, over
In your leef, life, loaf
See the deevel, divel, dovel
Kiss his weef, wife, woaf?

No, I neever, niver, nover
In my leef, life, loaf
Saw the deevel, divel, dovel
Kiss his weef, wife, woaf.

Anonymous

Auk Talk

The raucous auk must squawk to talk.
The squawk auks squawk to talk goes

Mary Ann Hoberman

Notice to Myself

Don't procrastinate:
it's time to vacate
shilly-shallying
dilly-dallying
idling sidling
ambling rambling
piddling fiddling
twiddling diddling
doodling noodling
and get right down to
non-shirk
work.

Eve Merriam

I Wave Good-bye When Butter Flies

I wave good-bye when butter flies
and cheer a boxing match,
I've often watched my pillow fight,
I've sewn a cabbage patch,
I like to dance at basket balls
or lead a rubber band,
I've marvelled at a spelling bee,
I've helped a peanut stand.

It's possible a pencil points,
but does a lemon drop?
Does coffee break or chocolate kiss,
and will a soda pop?
I share my milk with drinking straws,
my meals with chewing gum,
and should I see my pocket change,
I'll hear my kettle drum.

It makes me sad when lettuce leaves,
I laugh when dinner rolls,
I wonder if the kitchen sinks
and if a salad bowls,
I've listened to a diamond ring,
I've waved a football fan,
and if a chimney sweeps the floor,
I'm sure the garbage can.

Jack Prelutsky

3 * SPECIAL KINDS OF POETRY

Limericks

Takeoffs

Songs

Show-and-Spell Poems

Finders-Keepers Poems

Haiku

LIMERICKS

How the limerick began is uncertain. This kind of poem has the same name as a city in Ireland, but whether or not the first limericks came from Limerick, nobody knows. A limerick is a funny five-line poem in which the rhymes and rhythms are arranged like this:

> A bridge engineer, Mr. Crumpett,
> Built a bridge for the good River Bumpett.
>   A mistake in the plan
>   Left a gap in the span,
> But he said, "Well, they'll just have to jump it."
>
> *Anonymous*

The rhythm gallops. Long lines one, two, and five rhyme; so do shorter lines three and four.

Limericks started appearing in the early 1800s, but the form didn't become famous until Edward Lear wrote *The Book of Nonsense* in 1846. Here's one of his productions:

> There was an old person of Skye,
> Who waltz'd with a Bluebottle fly:
>   They buzz'd a sweet tune,
>   To the light of the moon,
> And entranced all the people of Skye.

Usually, Lear echoed the first line in the last line that way.

The limerick has gone on to be the most popular kind of poem in the English language. At least there are probably more limericks than any other kind. How come?

Well, it's partly the shape of the thing
That makes the old limerick swing—
   Its accordion pleats
   Full of light, airy beats
Take it up like a kite on the wing!

Anonymous

How awkward while playing with glue
To suddenly find out that you
   Have stuck nice and tight
   Your left hand to your right
In a permanent how-do-you-do!

Constance Levy

April Fool

At show-and-tell time yesterday
I brought my pet skunk. Sad to say,
   Though it had been well taught
   Not to spray, it forgot.
Now we can't use the schoolhouse till May.

John Ciardi

A piggish young person from Leeds
Made a meal on six packets of seeds
    But it soon came to pass
    That he broke out in grass
And he couldn't sit down for the weeds.

Anonymous

There was a young lady from Lynn
Who became so incredibly thin
    That in bringing her lip
    To some Coke for a sip
She slid down through the straw and fell in.

Anonymous

There was a Young Lady named Rose
Who was constantly blowing her nose;
    Because of this failing
    They sent her off whaling
So the whalers could say: "Thar she blows!"

William Jay Smith

There was a young lady of Twickenham
Whose shoes were too tight to walk quick in 'em.
　　She came back from her walk
　　Looking white as a chalk
And took 'em both off and was sick in 'em.

Oliver Herford

There was an old man from Peru
Who dreamed he was eating his shoe.
　　In the midst of the night
　　He awoke in a fright
And—good grief! it was perfectly true!

Anonymous

Blessèd Lord, what it is to be young:
To be of, to be for, be among—
   Be enchanted, enthralled,
   Be the caller, the called,
The singer, the song, and the sung.

                    David McCord

TAKEOFFS

Sometimes it's fun, when you're singing a song or saying a poem, to make changes in it.

Just for the nonsense of it, you substitute a word or two of your own for a word or two of the poet's. So, "Mary had a little lamb" becomes "Aladdin had a little lamp." You're well on your way to writing a takeoff—also called a parody.

A favorite poem to take off from is "The Star" by Jane Taylor. It begins:

> Twinkle, twinkle, little star,
> How I wonder what you are,
> Up above the world so high,
> Like a diamond in the sky.

Lewis Carroll, the author of *Alice in Wonderland*, made these playful changes in it:

> Twinkle, twinkle, little bat!
> How I wonder what you're at!
> Up above the world you fly,
> Like a tea tray in the sky.

Some writers of takeoffs don't merely change words. They will write a whole new poem from the beginning, as the first poet might have written it, only about something nutty.

Like somebody who dresses up in somebody else's clothes and does a little clowning, the writer of such a takeoff is borrowing the other poet's style. For instance, here's a famous poem in a simple style, easy to borrow:

This Is Just to Say

I have eaten
the plums
that were in
the icebox

and which
you were probably
saving
for breakfast

Forgive me
they were delicious
so sweet
and so cold

William Carlos Williams

Williams, by the way, was a doctor—a fact that Kenneth Koch re-
members in writing these takeoffs:

Variations on a Theme by
William Carlos Williams

1.
I chopped down the house that you had been saving to live
   in next summer.
I am sorry, but it was morning, and I had nothing to do
and its wooden beams were so inviting.

2.

We laughed at the hollyhocks together
and then I sprayed them with lye.
Forgive me. I simply do not know what I am doing.

3.

I gave away the money that you had been saving to live on
   for the next ten years.
The man who asked for it was shabby
and the firm March wind on the porch was so juicy and
   cold.

4.

Last evening we went dancing and I broke your leg.
Forgive me. I was clumsy, and
I wanted you here in the wards, where I am the doctor.

Kenneth Koch

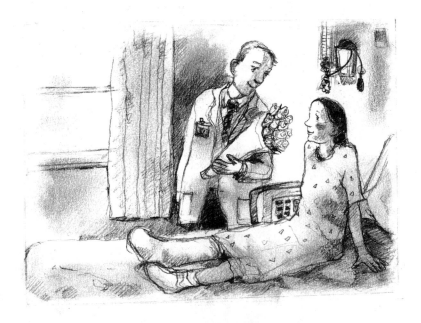

Clementine

In a cavern, in a canyon,
　　Excavating for a mine
Lived a miner, forty-niner,
　　And his daughter, Clementine.

Oh, my darling, oh, my darling,
　　Oh, my darling Clementine,
You are lost and gone forever,
　　Dreadful sorry, Clementine.

Anonymous
(American popular song)

In a cavern, in a canyon

In a cavern, in a canyon
　　Lay an unexpected mine.
Don't know where, Dear. DO TAKE CARE, DEAR . . .
　　Dreadful sorry, Clementine.

Paul Dehn

Sometimes in writing a takeoff, a poet ends up with a very different kind of poem. Here, for instance, are a nursery rhyme, "Sing a Song of Sixpence," which perhaps you already know, and a takeoff on it, "Sing a Song of Subways." Eve Merriam's takeoff begins like the famous nonsensical nursery rhyme, but it isn't about a king and a queen and a hot blackbird pie. It's about daily life in a big city, and it isn't nonsensical at all.

Sing a Song of Sixpence

Sing a song of sixpence,
A pocket full of rye,
Four and twenty blackbirds
Baked in a pie.

When the pie was opened
The birds began to sing—
Wasn't that a dainty dish
To set before the king?

The king was in the counting-house
Counting out his money,
The queen was in the parlor
Eating bread and honey,

The maid was in the garden
Hanging out the clothes.
Along came a blackbird
And snipped off her nose.

Anonymous

Sing a Song of Subways

Sing a song of subways,
Never see the sun;
Four-and-twenty people
In room for one.

When the doors are opened—
Everybody run.

Eve Merriam

Do you recognize the original for this next takeoff? It has been sung by Scottish children on the streets of Edinburgh.

We four lads

We four lads from Liverpool are:
Paul in a taxi, John in a car,
George on a scooter, tootin' his hooter,
Following Ringo Starr!

Anonymous

SONGS

Back whenever poetry began, it was probably sung. In ancient Greece, poems were sung to the strumming of a lyre, a stringed instrument. In the Bible, you find a collection of songs—the book of Psalms. (The word *psalm* comes from a Greek word meaning "the twanging of a harp.") In the middle ages, kings and other lords kept minstrels—poets and musicians—to play and sing for them. And people made up ballads, songs that told stories. People have always liked songs. Don't you?

In the fifteenth century, when the German printer and inventor Johannes Gutenberg made it possible to print books on a printing press, he worked great changes. Books no longer needed to be copied by hand, and poets could share their poems without twanging a harp anymore. Ever since the year 1620 or so, most poems have been written to be read on a page. But there are still plenty of poems to sing, both new and old.

Some popular songs you hear on the radio or on CD's are poems, but not all. If you just read their lyrics (the words without the music) from a song sheet or CD notes, sometimes the words will seem silly, as thin and forgettable as last night's bathwater. There's no reason why a good song *has* to be poetry, of course. You can sing any song and take pleasure in it. But if its words contain vivid images and likenesses and word music, then the song also gives you the special pleasure of poetry.

You've already met some singable poems: "John Henry," "Clementine," and "We four lads." Now here are other poems to sing. Some tell stories; some tell how the singer feels. One reward in singing is that you may find yourself feeling the same way. Maybe that's why everyone likes glad songs. But aren't there times when a sad song—or a moody song—expresses just what you need to feel?

Here's a favorite of folksingers. It's a modern version of an English song that's more than five hundred years old.

Riddle Song

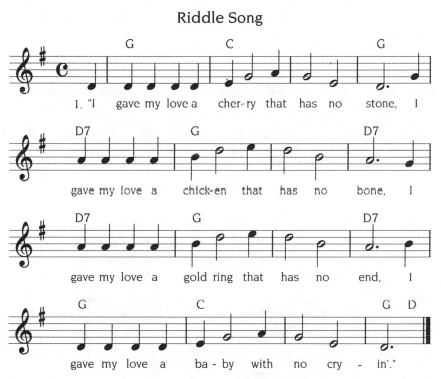

1. "I gave my love a cher-ry that has no stone, I gave my love a chick-en that has no bone, I gave my love a gold ring that has no end, I gave my love a ba-by with no cry-in'."

2 How can there be a cherry that has no stone?
How can there be a chicken that has no bone?
How can there be a gold ring that has no end?
How can there be a baby with no cryin'?

3 A cherry when it's blooming, it has no stone.
A chicken in the eggshell, it has no bone.
A gold ring when it's rolling, it has no end.
A baby when it's sleeping has no cryin'.

Anonymous
(Melody and guitar chords transcribed
by John Jacob Niles)

Another song, "I Had a Little Nut Tree," has also proved to be long lasting. Some think it tells how the king of Spain's daughter, Juana of Castile, came to England in the year 1506 to visit King Henry VII. Whether or not the poet had Juana and Henry in mind, his words have been set to cheerful music that you may have heard before.

I Had a Little Nut Tree

Anonymous
(*Transcribed by Daniel J. Kennedy*)

In the earlier days of America, busy wagons carried tools, cloth, and groceries from the East Coast into the Great Smoky Mountains of Tennessee. Some mountain women fell in love with wagon-driving men. In this song, the man goes off, leaving the woman feeling bitter and alone. "On Top of Old Smoky" is one of the most popular American folk songs ever. It has often been sung to a slowly picked banjo, but a piano or guitar (or just your voice) will certainly work, too.

On Top of Old Smoky

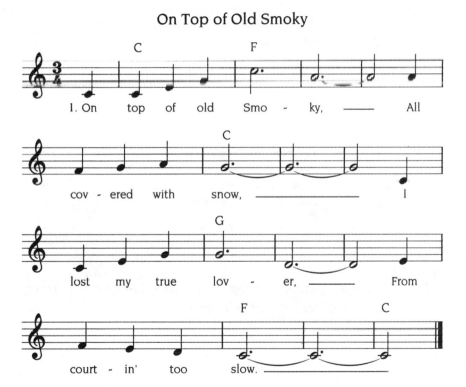

2 Now, courtin's a pleasure,
   But parting is grief,
   And a false-hearted lover
   Is worse than a thief;

3 For a thief will just rob you
   And take what you have,
   But a false-hearted lover
   Will lead you to the grave;

4 And the grave will decay you,
   And turn you to dust.
   Not one boy in a hundred
   A poor girl can trust:

5 They'll hug you and kiss you,
   And tell you more lies
   Than the crossties on a railroad,
   Or stars in the skies.

6 So, come all you young maidens,
   And listen to me:
   Never place your affections
   In a green willow tree;

7 For the leaves they will wither,
   And the roots they will die.
   Your lover will forsake you,
   And you'll never know why.

Anonymous

Finally, here is a famous modern song, one that voices a strong wish for peace and freedom for all people.

Blowin' in the Wind

2 How many times must a man look up
before he can see the sky?
Yes, 'n' how many ears must one man have
before he can hear people cry?
Yes, 'n' how many deaths will it take till he knows
that too many people have died?
  The answer, my friend, is blowin' in the wind,
  The answer is blowin' in the wind.

3 How many years can a mountain exist
before it's washed to the sea?
Yes, 'n' how many years can some people exist
before they're allowed to be free?
Yes, 'n' how many times can a man turn his head
pretending he just doesn't see?
  The answer, my friend, is blowin' in the wind,
  The answer is blowin' in the wind.
  The answer is blowin' in the wind.

Bob Dylan

SHOW-AND-SPELL POEMS

Good poetry is music to our ears. Sometimes poems please our
eyes as well.

The Dancing Bear

Slowly he turns himself round and round,
   Lifting his paws with care,
Twisting his head in a sort of bow
   To the people watching there.

His keeper, grinding a wheezy tune,
   Jerks at the iron chain,
And the dusty, patient bear goes through
   His solemn tricks again.

Only his eyes are still and fixed
   In a wide, bewildered stare,
More like a child's lost in woods at night
   Than the eyes of a big brown bear.

Rachel Field

Why does this poem look neat? Why is it three shapes in a stack?
Because the poet wrote it in stanzas, or clusters of lines joined with

rhyme. On paper, Rachel Field has arranged her poem to show the rhyming lines. She indents them—that is, she pushes them in. And she leaves white space between the three stanzas.

Stanzas can also result from singing words to music. To prove this to yourself, try writing down the words of a song you know by heart or have a recording of. End every line on a rhyme word. Group together each bunch of lines that rhyme. You'll get stanzas.

Other poems may look more loosely scattered. They may be set on the page unevenly, like flowers in a vase:

**You
Can Talk About Your Hummingbirds**

on hot june afternoons   sticking
                        noses

into sweet clematis blooms
and
talk about goldfinch feathers
      against green leaves
but
during winter
     winter mornings
we are
   the gray birds of the yards

     sometimes in march
  the only moving
      things on frozen
         air

Arnold Adoff

Here the poet may be trying to make certain words stand out. And if you read the poem aloud, pausing on the white spaces, those words may seem to matter all the more. This poem uses words to say something while arranging the words in an eye-pleasing way.

One way a poet can please the eye is to place words in shapes, for the fun of it. Like this:

**The Sidewalk Racer
Or, On the Skateboard**

Skimming
an asphalt sea
I swerve, I curve, I
sway; I speed to whirring
sound an inch above the
ground; I'm the sailor
and the sail, I'm the
driver and the wheel
I'm the one and only
single engine
human auto
mobile

Lillian Morrison

The previous poem, "The Sidewalk Racer," looks like what it's *about*. It's fun to see. (Being written with rhythm and rhyme, it's also fun to hear.)

In this next poem, the poet is trying to show us not a solid object, but a motion. How well do you think he succeeds?

Ian Hamilton Finlay

Fury said to a mouse

Fury said to
a mouse, That
he met
in the
house,
"Let us
both go
to law:
I will
prosecute
you. —
Come, I'll
take no
denial;
We must
have a
trial:
For
really
this
morning
I've
nothing
to do."
Said the
mouse to
the cur,
"Such a
trial,
dear sir,
With no
jury or
judge,
would be
wasting
our breath."
"I'll be
judge.
I'll be
jury,"
Said
cunning
old Fury:
"I'll try
the whole
cause,
and
condemn
you
to
death."

Lewis Carroll

Seashells

Seashells
scattered
on
the
whistle   shore,
they   songs,   swept
long   retired   there
day   on   by
all   the   the
But   beach.   ocean,
reach.   once
or   held
leap   creatures
cannot   deep
creep,   inside,
cannot   creeping
seashells   in
Empty   slow-motion.

Douglas Florian

For a Quick Exit

For going up or coming down,
in big department stores in town,
you take an escalator.
(They come in pairs.)
Or else an elevator.
(Also stairs.)

I wish storekeepers would provide

    a
     s
      l
       i
      d
       e
        !

Norma Farber

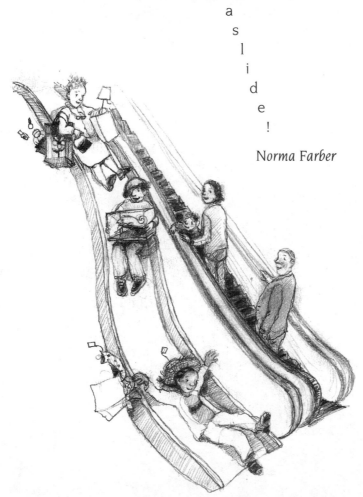

Concrete Cat

```
        A          A
      e   r      e   r


                         stripestripestripestripe   t
    eYe     eYe              stripestripestripe       a i l  t a i l
 whisker  m   h whisker       stripestripestripestripe
 whisker    o   t  whisker       stripestripestripe
              U            stripestripestripestripe


            paw  paw          paw  paw              ɘsnoɯ

   dishdish                                litterbox
                                           litterbox
```

Dorthi Charles

HANDSAWWWWWWWWWWWWWWWWW

Richard Lebovitz

FINDERS-KEEPERS POEMS

Poetry is all around us, sometimes in words we hardly bother to hear. We'll catch a striking phrase ("That new baby is bright as a new penny") or an unusual name ("Spanish Fork, Utah") or an old saying ("Red sky at night is the sailor's delight," "The grass is always greener on the other side of the fence"), and we'll realize with a start that we've heard a bit of poetry. Once in a while you see some words, not in a book, that don't claim to be poetry—and yet seem to be. They say something that makes you think and feel about it. There's something to remember in the very sound of the words. Here's a sign that used to stand at the entrance to Great Meadows National Wildlife Sanctuary in Concord, Massachusetts:

> GATE
> UNLOCKS
> AT SUNRISE
> LIFT
> GENTLY
> TO OPEN

Nobody calls that sign a poem, but isn't it as good a poem as many?

Some poets look for poetry ready-made in the world around them, even in some places that don't seem promising: traffic signs, restaurant menus, recipes in cookbooks, labels on soup cans, billboards. Sometimes all the poet has to do is put the words into a new arrangement, as Ronald Gross does in the poem on the next page.

Yield

Yield.
No Parking.
Unlawful to Pass.
Wait for Green Light.
Yield.

Stop.
Narrow Bridge.
Merging Traffic Ahead.
Yield.

Yield.

Ronald Gross

You can see why such a poem is called a "found" poem. What did Gross make it out of? (Try reading it out loud, as if you're mad at somebody.)

Dorothy Wordsworth wrote these words in her journal. More than a century later, a scholar found them, liked them, arranged them in lines, and declared that Dorothy's brother William wasn't the only poet in the Wordsworth family.

The lake was covered all over

The lake was covered all over
With bright silverwaves
That were each
The twinkling of an eye.

Dorothy Wordsworth

4-Way Stop

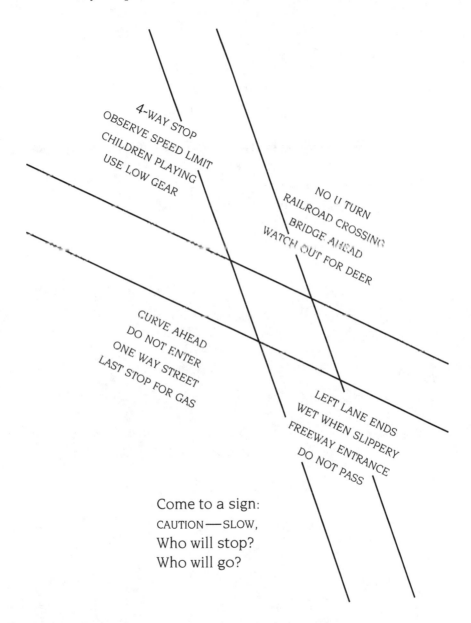

4-WAY STOP
OBSERVE SPEED LIMIT
CHILDREN PLAYING
USE LOW GEAR

NO U TURN
RAILROAD CROSSING
BRIDGE AHEAD
WATCH OUT FOR DEER

CURVE AHEAD
DO NOT ENTER
ONE WAY STREET
LAST STOP FOR GAS

LEFT LANE ENDS
WET WHEN SLIPPERY
FREEWAY ENTRANCE
DO NOT PASS

Come to a sign:
CAUTION — SLOW,
Who will stop?
Who will go?

Myra Cohn Livingston

141

Genuine Poem,
Found on a Blackboard
in a Bowling Alley
in Story City, Iowa

If you strike
when head pin
is red pin,
one free game
to each line.
Notify desk
before you throw
if head pin
is red

Ted Kooser

HAIKU

Haiku, which began in Japan, are short poems that keep you thinking and feeling for longer than they take to read. Because haiku may have started out as a game, the name means "beginning-verse." Players, given a haiku, were supposed to go on and make a longer poem out of it. But some haiku came to be well known, short as they are. Here are some Japanese haiku in translation:

> Ancient pool. Sound
> of a frog's leap—
> Splisssssshhhhh. . . .
>
> *Bashō*
> (*Translated by Olivia Gray*)

> A bantam rooster
> spreading his ruff of feathers
> thinks he's a lion!
>
> *Kikaku*
> (*Translated by Harry Behn*)

In Japanese, haiku are just seventeen syllables long. If you're writing a haiku in English, though, you don't have to keep exactly to that count. The main thing is to keep it short and, if possible, in three lines. Because the poem is so brief, you don't have room to talk about your feelings. You just point to something and let it make the reader (or listener) feel something, too. A good haiku, tossed out into your reader's mind, should go on and on—like the waves from the frog's leap into the pool.

Now the swing is still:
  a suspended tire
    centers the autumn moon.

Nicholas Virgilio

out after dark . . .
chasing flashlight circles
across the grass

Penny Harter

midnight sirens—
three dogs howl
in harmony

Penny Harter

Tunnel

Tunnel in the park:
a sandwich of night between
two slices of light.

Sylvia Cassedy

The green cockleburs
Caught in the thick wooly hair
Of the black boy's head

Richard Wright

After weeks of watching the roof leak
I fixed it tonight
by moving a single board.

Gary Snyder

Bang! the starter's gun —
thin raindrops
sprint.

Dorthi Charles

August

At bedtime, outside
my room . . . nighthawk and trainsong
on the wind's guitar.

J. *Patrick Lewis*

4 * DO IT YOURSELF

Writing Your Own Poems
Ideas

Writing Your Own Poems

Maybe browsing among the poems in this book has inspired you to try writing some. Whether or not you are a gifted poet, you can have fun writing verse of your own. Find a quiet place to work; then be lazy and let your ideas play. You need very little equipment — just paper and a pencil or pen.

Watch a first grader building a castle with a set of wooden blocks. He piles up some big, smooth, cube-shaped ones and puts a cone or pyramid on top. He knocks them down and starts over. He finds just the right cylinder for a turret, and he tops that with a cone-shaped roof. He knocks down the bridge over the moat because he has found a bigger block that will make a stronger bridge. He is enjoying himself thoroughly.

In much the same way, a poet likes to build playfully with words. He may begin with a few good-sounding ones. He crosses them out and substitutes better ones. He moves a whole line from the top of the page to the bottom. He reads a line aloud and adds a word. He is having a fine old time. And, if he is a good poet, he ends up with a stronger poem than the one he began. Poems not only can be fun to write; they can be fun to improve.

There are, it is true, a few dangers to avoid as you start putting words down on paper. Say you have just read "An Autumn Song," by Bliss Carman, which starts out:

> The scarlet of the maples can shake me like a cry
> Of bugles going by.

You might think, "That's beautiful! I want to write something just like it!" And then you may plunge into your own tribute to red leaves. But stop and think. Does the sight of leaves on a tree really and truly affect you deeply? If red leaves don't make you feel much of anything, *don't pretend*. Phony baloney = bad poetry.

A not-very-good poet once wrote:

> In the prison cell we sit—
> Are we broken-hearted? Nit!

In those lines, the rhyme is giving orders to the poet instead of the other way around. Very likely, what the writer *wanted* to say was:

> In the prison cell we sit—
> Are we broken-hearted? No!

but he felt he had to force his poem to rhyme. If you face a choice between rhyming and saying what you mean, it is a whole lot better to say what you mean.

Poems don't have to be solemn and serious, either. A sense of humor is as welcome in a poet as in anyone else.

If you'd like to write a poem, but don't know how to begin, here are a few suggestions to help you get started.

Ideas

1. Find a few words or sentences you have read and want to remember—a statement that strikes you as strange or funny or beautiful, or perhaps unusual-sounding. You might find this in a newspaper or magazine story, in ads, in schoolbooks, or just about anywhere else. Try arranging the words into a poem, like the "found poems" on pages 139 to 142.

2. Take another look at the show-and-spell poems on pages 131 to 138. Then try writing a shaped poem of your own. First pick a small object with a simple shape everybody can recognize: a star, a bird, a pyramid, an ice cream cone. (A large, complicated shape, such as a football team or a stegosaurus, might be pretty hard to build out of words.) Then write a short poem about that object, not worrying yet about the shape. When you have your poem the way you want it, pencil the shape on a piece of paper and try writing or typing the words into it.

3. Maybe you are familiar with:

   > Teddy bear, teddy bear, turn around,
   > Teddy bear, teddy bear, touch the ground,
   > Teddy bear, teddy bear, show your shoe,
   > Teddy bear, teddy bear, out go you!

This and a lot of other jump-rope rhymes have been chanted by generations of jumpers. Can you write a new one? Don't forget to try it out on the playground!

To help you get started, here's a new jump-rope rhyme made up by Eloise Greenfield:

Rope Rhyme

Get set, ready now, jump right in
Bounce and kick and giggle and spin
Listen to the rope when it hits the ground
Listen to that clappedy-slappedy sound
Jump right up when it tells you to
Come back down, whatever you do
Count to a hundred, count by ten
Start to count all over again
That's what jumping is all about
Get set, ready now,

> jump
>> right
>>> out!

4. Write a nonsense poem. If you don't know how to start, try a limerick. (For examples, see pages 113 to 117.) Your first line might go something like, "There was a young someone from someplace." Then keep going—find another line to rhyme with that, then two more lines and a last line, and you'll have it made.

5. Write a takeoff on any poem you like. Or don't like.

6. Write a poem in which you describe a person you know, a favorite place, an animal, or a thing. Then see whether a friend can recognize your subject from reading your poem. (If your friend is your subject, you'd better make your description friendly, not insulting. You don't want to lose your friend.)

7. Write a poem that appeals to one of your five senses: taste, smell, touch, sight, or hearing. (See pages 63 to 70 for some poems that make such appeals.)

8. Have you had an experience or a feeling you'd like to share? Write it into a poem, as Judith Viorst did:

That Old Haunted House

That old haunted house was so creepy, so crawly, so ghastly,
    so ghostly, so gruesome, so skully-and-bony.
That old haunted house gave me nightmares and daymares and
    shudders and shivers and quivers and quavers and quakes.
That old haunted house made my hair stand on end and my
    heart pound-pound-pound and the blood in my veins ice-
    cold-freezing.
That old haunted house gave me goose bumps and throat lumps
    and ch-ch-ch-chattering teeth and the sh-sh-sh-shakes.
That old haunted house made me shriek, made me eeek, made
    me faint, made me scared-to-death scared, made me all-over
    sweat.
Would I ever go back to that old haunted house?
You bet.

9. If you have a computer you can use, try writing a poem right on screen. Play around with the poem — moving the lines, trying other words — until you get it just as good as it can be. You'll find a computer a very useful tool for writing a poem in rhyme or in some tricky form like a limerick. Such poems often need a lot of playing around with before they turn out right. With a computer, when you have a line that needs to rhyme, you can always write a few different lines, each ending in a different rhyme. Then you decide which line sounds best and wipe out the others — ZAP!

10. After you've read the haiku on pages 143 to 146, try one of your own. Remember, it doesn't need to rhyme. Just keep it down to three short lines. Begin with something you've actually seen or heard or touched or smelled or tasted. A haiku doesn't have room to let you blab about your feelings. You can't say,

> Oh, poor me!
> Nobody likes me.
> How sad I am.

or you'll use up all your space. Some haiku poets start with one image, then add another that acts together with the first:

> On the one-ton temple bell
> a butterfly, folded into sleep,
> sits still.

In this haiku by Bashō, when these two oddly matched things meet (bell weighing a ton, frail butterfly), the effect on the reader is a little surprise. It is almost as though the heavy bell had rung.

Do It Yourself

Buy our little magazine
Quite the smallest ever seen
Printed on a square of tissue
Just
One
Letter
In
Each
Issue.
With each issue, given free
A seed pearl and a pinch of tea.

Thread the seed pearl, save the pinch,
Make a necklace, inch by inch,
Fill a warehouse, ton by ton,
Save the letters, one by one,
Lay
The
Letters
In
A
Row
Make the rhyme you're reading now

Joan Aiken

Whether you're a poet or not, you can have great fun trying to write your own poems. Of course, sometimes you may feel like tearing out your hair when a rhyme won't come or a line won't turn out right. But at least your own efforts may help you appreciate good poets and good poetry and show you why the best poems are worth remembering. If that happens to you, you will have discovered a treasure. After all, shooting baskets yourself is one way to appreciate the skill of the players in the NBA who can sink a basket almost every time.

And who knows? To write a poem that you'll want to keep may give you great satisfaction your whole life long. Then perhaps you'll see what Robert Herrick meant when, more than three hundred and fifty years ago, he likened the joy of writing a poem to being crowned with roses. He prayed that he might write another poem,

> And once more yet (ere I am laid out dead)
> Knock at a star with my exalted head.

Afterword to Adults

About This Book

Knock at a Star is addressed directly to children from eight to twelve, give or take a year or two — those who can read for themselves and care to do so. The book may simply be placed in their hands, allowing them to decide whether or not to get involved with it. To be sure, whatever encouragement the giver can provide may well prove invaluable.

We gathered poems that we have found to amuse, delight, and engage children in third grade through sixth. We have tried to leave out what children "ought" to like. In some anthologies of olden days and in some still current, unrealistic views of a child's attention span prevail. Some anthologists let in the more trivial and forgettable efforts of Shakespeare, Milton, and other great writers, or represent them by little snippets out of longer poems. We work in the faith that, to a child, resounding names matter less than graspable poems. A few great names have found their way into this book, but they are attached to poems that children usually like. We suspect that those poems that children can't at least partly understand aren't likely to stick with them. We assume that children who learn to love poems they see eye to eye with may go on later to poems of greater complexity.

Except for a couple of excerpts inserted as examples, we have chosen whole poems originally written in English. This is a great age for verse translation, but the vast resources of poetry in English seem enough to represent in so short an introduction. An exception has been made in the section on haiku, a form best demonstrated with the aid of some translations from the Japanese.

Since 1982, when the first edition of this book appeared, a new growth of interest in poetry for children has burgeoned. New poets have arrived, and many bright new anthologies. Poetry has reasserted its place in schoolbooks, reading aloud has been demonstrated to increase literacy, and the influential California Reading Initiative has included much more poetry in its lists of essential books for children's libraries. To reflect this fresh excitement, we have tried to bring *Knock at a Star* up to the eve of the twenty-first century. We have added seventy-five new poems, while retaining 104 well-liked poems from the first edition. Some of the prose has been substantially rewritten and updated. But the thrust of the book—to appeal to children directly—is no different from what it used to be.

Encouraging Children to Like Poetry

Lucky is the child whose closest adults like to read poetry. Luckier still is the child who from earliest years has listened to poems read or sung. By the time they can read for themselves, such children are already at home with poetry.

People who wish their children to grow up liking poetry will do well, we believe, to start reading aloud to them as soon as they can sit up and help turn pages. Whether the text be Mother Goose or Dr. Seuss, there is nothing like a warm lap or an enclosing arm and a friendly voice to help a child learn to love words.

For the children, more than mere fondness for poetry is at stake. There is a close correlation between a child's reading skills and whether that child enjoys books instead of television shows as bedtime rewards. You can do children a great service by reading to them every day, even for fifteen minutes. And why stop after they've learned how to read for themselves? Even for readers, hearing language read aloud continues to nourish literacy.

At times when you're hopelessly busy, or not available, you might try having an older child read to a younger; in a one-child family, you might enlist the baby-sitter. (The older child or the sitter may reap as many rewards from the experience as the audience.)

With or without an early start, most children, even those of eight or older, will respond with enthusiasm to vigorous, plainspoken poetry. As William Stafford remarks of children (in his "Keepsakes"),

> They dance before they learn
> there is anything that isn't music.

Despite competition from video screens, skipping ropes continue to twirl, filling the air not only with jumpers but with timeless jingles:

> Grace, Grace, dressed in lace,
> Went upstairs to powder her face.
> How many boxes did she use?
> One, two, three . . .

It is later, usually in junior high or high school, that a distaste for poetry sets in like winter frost. It tends to arrive when children are obliged to discuss poems in class, sometimes at great length, or when they're assigned to write papers about poems. They come to suspect that the meaning of a poem is a secret, the exclusive property of teachers. Before that grim suspicion strikes, caring adults may help children realize that poetry is fun—and revelation. (For those teachers who already regard poetry as a joy, and they are legion, we include a few suggestions "For People Who Work With Groups," page 163.)

Children love nonsense, but often the poems they like will take in any kind of reality whatsoever. Many of our selections state values—for instance, James Hayford's "Time to Plant Trees," or Hal Summers's "My Old Cat"—but we shy away from poems that moralize. In general, we have sought poems whose language is direct and contemporary, poems that, however short, brim with energy. We wanted feelingful poems, vivid and concrete in images, rhythmic, rich in sound, and whenever possible, graced with a bit of magic.

That children love to scrutinize things at close range — anthills and animals, grasshoppers and gyroscopes — persuades us that, with a little encouragement, they may care to look closely at poems as well. To invite young readers to analyze poems, we know, flies in the face of much expert advice. A widely held assumption is that if you ask children to look closely at a poem, you will kill whatever pleasure they may take in it. You're asking them to tear the wings off a delicate butterfly. Indeed, we share the view that too much analysis can be self-defeating. There is something wrong with (as poet Elizabeth Bishop once said) "making poetry monstrous or boring and proceeding to talk the very life out of it." And yet we believe just as strongly that what is inside a good poem may interest children greatly. Butterflies can be inspected without ripping them apart. Children like to learn the rules of games, and poetry, in its forms and measures, has gamelike elements. So we wouldn't be afraid to point out a thing or two we've noticed within a poem — even a rhythm or a rhyme scheme — and to invite kids to point out anything curious that they may have noticed, too.

Nor do we accept the notion that every child is a born poet whose every utterance deserves praise. Most poems, whether written by children or adults, are chaff for the wind to drive away. Still, we include a chapter on writing poems. In feeling their way into poetry, children have much to learn from trying to write it. At least they may discover that good poetry is hard to write, and so may relish all the more what the best poets have accomplished. If any of them should turn out to be good poets themselves, that would be wonderful.

To encourage reading and borrowing, it helps to set out a bunch of poetry books of wildly different kinds. Let the kids page through them, and choose for themselves which ones they want to read. For lists of some books that might tempt them, see Zena Sutherland's *Children and Books*, ninth edition (Longman, 1997), Judy Freeman's *Books Kids Will Sit Still For*, second edition (Bowker, 1990), and *More Books Kids Will Sit Still For* (Bowker, 1997). For opinions on latest books, see current issues of *The Horn Book*, *Bulletin of the Center for Children's Books*, and *School Library Journal*.

Any introduction to the Muse, of course, may leave some young readers feeling, "Aw, so what?" This natural reaction need not discourage you. Not all adults care for poetry, either, yet most manage to be useful citizens. Poetry may not be able to redeem the world, but it offers lasting satisfactions. It can sharpen the wits, fire the imagination, perhaps even leave the reader with a grain of wisdom. It can heighten the experience of being alive. This seems enough to ask of it.

When Kids Write Their Own Poems

Here are a few suggestions for inviting children to write poetry:

1. Before having children write, have them read and hear good poems.

2. If they seem willing to learn any poems by heart, encourage them to go to it.

3. Make clear to them that poems don't need to rhyme. But if their poems *want* to rhyme, let them.

4. In your suggestions for writing, offer choices. Your suggestions don't have to list possible subjects to write about. Poems may begin from anything: not only a subject, but a word, a feeling, an experience.

5. Don't wax enthusiastic over mediocre stuff. Don't be afraid to offer a kind suggestion for improvement or to wonder about a line you can't understand. Just don't smother your budding bards with nit-picking technical advice.

6. When you read a child's poem in group discussion, it's a good idea to invite other children in the group to express their reactions. Cut short any prolonged tearing-apart of poems. Ask not just for faultfinding; ask which parts of a poem listeners *like*, thus providing the poet with the encouragement of public acclaim (if any).

7. If you oblige children to haul out pencils and write on the spot for five or ten minutes, don't expect the results to be miraculous. Some poets are slow thinkers and need time to rewrite. Urge children to keep working on their poems, with the understanding that they can show their finished versions to the group at a later time. Invite them to take their unfinished poems home with them.

8. Provide some form of publication. A photocopied two-sheet poetry magazine might inspire contributors. Access to a computer, to type in one's poem and have it available on screen for others to read, might also encourage young poets. At the very least, you can display some of the poems on walls or on a bulletin board. Or have the children bind their poems into booklets with illustrated covers, and make this instant library available to all.

9. After children have written a few poems, stage a poetry reading, with each child (unless unwilling) taking part. The audience can be the other participants, possibly including their families and friends. It might be doubly rewarding to the poets to film this event with a camcorder and screen the results. (We'll offer some suggestions for poetry readings in the next section.)

For People Who Work with Groups

For those teachers who wish to bring this book to class, for librarians who work with reading groups, for poets who visit schools, and for parents or other adults who wish to start a group of children reading poetry, here are a few suggestions.

Because good poems are made of well-chosen words, there is nothing better than reading them aloud. Before reading to a group, however, an inexperienced adult had better practice. Every reader-aloud of poetry needs to understand what a poem is saying and needs to share some of the poet's apparent feelings. A tape recorder, so you can hear yourself, may be helpful; and if children are encouraged to read aloud, too, they may enjoy hearing their own readings on tape. A temptation to avoid—and it is one into which groups of kids tend to fall, when given a metrical, regularly rhythmic poem—is to read in a singsong chant, which renders the poem monotonous and feelingless. Read with some oomph yourself: at least, whatever oomph you honestly feel. Don't be afraid to ham it up, within reason. Children aren't stern drama critics. (Incidentally, it may be worth pointing out sometimes that there are some poems *not* meant to be read aloud: puzzling or difficult poems that take slow figuring-out; visual poems, like those in the "Show-and-Spell" section of this book.)

In reading aloud, it helps if children and adults group themselves together: not in a theatrical situation with the adult up front as if on pulpit or podium, but with everybody relaxed, sitting elbow to elbow, in a circle on the floor or in any close arrangement that is comfortable. With children of eight or nine, about twenty minutes of poetry reading at a stretch is usually plenty. Even adult poetry audiences seldom can listen to poetry for more than fifty minutes. Children will quickly alert you when they are restless; they will probably want to get up and run around. So don't oversupply them with material, and intersperse moments of relaxation and physical exercise.

Fine recordings of poets reading their works are available: Robert Frost, Dylan Thomas, E. E. Cummings, and Edna St. Vincent Millay are among the celebrated readers. However, while kids may be asked to do a brief amount of such listening, we find that only teenagers are likely to listen to recordings patiently for very long. Among the eight-to-twelve-year-olds, poetry works best when the listeners are given a chance to take part. One method is choral reading, in which the group members all read from a copy of a poem displayed on a card or chalkboard or projected slide (a device that probably brings people together more than if each reads from an individual copy). Here again, care needs to be taken lest a choral reading become a monotonous singsong. Some experienced teachers have reported good luck in using a poem full of repetitions: a chorus or refrain that the kids can speak together, while a single voice (perhaps the adult's) reads the other lines of the stanzas.

Some people like to use songs that have definite beats and ask the kids to clap to a rhythm. It's worth a try, but we admit we have never had much luck with it ourselves. The custom tends just to mess up the beat, as the clappers can't always agree on their timing. Anyhow, it is probably the meaning of the poem that needs stressing, not the regular beat, if any. The regular beat will make itself heard, but its effect is subtler than hand clapping. Those blessed with musical skills, who can bring in a guitar or a pair of castanets, can make kids aware that many poems are songs.

Children may be invited to illustrate the poems they hear — a playful activity that focuses their visual imaginations onto paper. Although we have no powerful convictions about this, we suspect it is probably better if the drawings are kept to simple sketches. Poems do much more than enter pictures in our heads; good poems suggest, perhaps indefinitely.

Ideally, children need to know the way to their local library and wear a path to its door. One impediment to their taking poetry home with them, however, seems to be the Dewey decimal system.

It buries poetry off in the 800's, remote from where children tend to look for recreational reading. The Library of Congress system can also erect barriers. Its ingenious system of call numbers seems not to have been invented with children in mind. All praise to those librarians who outwit Dewey and the Library of Congress by bringing a sheaf of poetry books out of the stacks and displaying them on a tempting, accessible table or shelf.

Should children be asked to memorize poetry? Those of us who have been required to memorize passages in grade school are sometimes astonished to realize how clearly certain poems or documents (Lincoln's Gettysburg Address, the Preamble to the Constitution) have remained in memory. Although nowhere in this book do we tell children to memorize long passages, we feel that the idea of learning things by heart deserves a fresh look. Some children can't memorize to save their necks and shouldn't be expected to; but we think it does no harm to ask a group—in the course of a happy and successful reading party—"Who can say that poem over again?" Or "Who can say a poem out loud? Any poem you remember." (You might be lucky enough to collect some living specimens of contemporary childhood folk poetry.) So employed, learning by heart isn't a grim chore, but another way to remind kids that poems aren't merely to be seen, but also to be heard—and cherished.

Working with groups of children, you never know what to expect—and that is part of the joy of it. Above all, be modest in your expectations. Don't feel that every child is duty-bound to love poetry. Don't blame yourself if some children receive it with ho-hums. Most children, at the very least, will stand for it—even enjoy a good part of it. And, seeing that you care for poetry yourself, most will want to share your pleasure in it.

Index of Authors

Index of Titles

Index of First Lines

Acknowledgments

For permission to include copyrighted material, we gratefully make the following acknowledgments.

Virginia Adair: "Key Ring" from *Ants on the Melon* by Virginia Adair. Copyright © 1996 by Virginia Hamilton Adair. Reprinted by permission of Random House, Inc.

Arnold Adoff: "You Can Talk About Your Hummingbirds" from *Birds: Poems by Arnold Adoff*. Text copyright ©1982 by Arnold Adoff. Used by permission of HarperCollins Publishers.

Joan Aiken: "Do It Yourself" from *The Skin Spinners* by Joan Aiken (Viking Press). Copyright © 1975 by Joan Aiken. Reprinted by permission of Brandt & Brandt Literary Agents, Inc.

A. R. Ammons: "Spruce Woods" from *The Hudson Review*. Reprinted by permission of the author.

Harry Behn: "A bantam rooster" from *More Cricket Songs: Japanese Haiku*, translated by Harry Behn. Copyright © 1971 by Harry Behn. Used by permission of Marian Reiner.

Stephen Vincent Benét: "Daniel Boone" from *A Book of Americans* by Rosemary and Stephen Vincent Benét (Henry Holt and Company). Copyright © 1933 by Rosemary and Stephen Vincent Benét. Copyright renewed © 1961 by Rosemary Carr Benét. Reprinted by permission of Brandt & Brandt Literary Agents, Inc.

Alan Benjamin: "Plant Life" from *A Nickel Buys a Rhyme* by Alan Benjamin. Copyright © 1993 by Alan Benjamin. Reprinted by permission of Greenwillow Books, a division of William Morrow & Company, Inc.

Morris Bishop: "Song of the Pop Bottlers" from *The New Yorker*, May 15, 1955. Reprinted by permission. Copyright © 1955 by Morris Bishop. Originally in *The New Yorker*. All rights reserved.

N. M. Bodecker: "Getting Together" from *Let's Marry Said the Cherry* by N. M. Bodecker. Reprinted by permission of Torsten Bodecker. "Sing Me a Song of Teapots and Trumpets" and "Mice Are Nice" reprinted with the permission of Margaret K. McElderry Books, an imprint of Simon & Schuster Children's Publishing Division from *Hurry, Hurry, Mary Dear! and Other Nonsense Poems* by N. M. Bodecker. Copyright © 1976 by N. M. Bodecker.

Richard Brautigan: "A Boat" and "Surprise" from *The Pill Versus the Springhill Mine Disaster*. Copyright © 1968 by Richard Brautigan. Reprinted by permission of Houghton Mifflin Company. All rights reserved.

Gwendolyn Brooks: "Narcissa" from *Bronzeville Boys and Girls* by Gwendolyn Brooks. "We Real Cool" from *Blacks* by Gwendolyn Brooks. Both reprinted by permission of the author.

Ashley Bryan: "Mama's Bouquets" from *Sing to the Sun* by Ashley Bryan. Copyright © 1992 by Ashley Bryan. Used by permission of HarperCollins Publishers.

Sylvia Cassedy: "Tunnel" from *Roomrimes* by Sylvia Cassedy (Thomas Y. Crowell Co., 1987). Copyright © by Sylvia Cassedy. Reprinted by permission of Ellen Cassedy.

Charles Causley: "What Has Happened to Lulu?" from *Charles Causley 1951–1975 Collected Poems* (David R. Godine). Reprinted by permission of Harold Ober Associates Inc.

Deborah Chandra: "Porch Light" from *Rich Lizard and Other Poems* by Deborah Chandra. Copyright © 1993 by Deborah Chandra. Reprinted by permission of Farrar, Straus & Giroux, Inc.

John Ciardi: "April Fool" from *The Hopeful Trout and Other Limericks* by John Ciardi. Text copyright © 1989 by Myra J. Ciardi. Reprinted by permission of Houghton Mifflin Company. All rights reserved. "Mummy Slept Late and Daddy Fixed Breakfast" from *You Read to Me, I'll Read to You* by John Ciardi. Copyright © 1962 by John Ciardi. Used by permission of HarperCollins Publishers.

Sandra Cisneros: "Good Hot Dogs/Buenos Hot Dogs" from *My Wicked Wicked Ways* in English and *Cool Salsa* in Spanish. Copyright © 1987 by Sandra Cisneros in English, published by Third Woman Press and in hardcover by Alfred A. Knopf, Inc. Copyright © 1994 by Sandra Cisneros in Spanish, published by Henry Holt and Company. Reprinted by permission of Susan Bergholz Literary Services, New York. All rights reserved.

Lucille Clifton: "the 1st" copyright © 1987 by Lucille Clifton. Reprinted from *Good Woman: Poems and a Memoir 1969–1980* with the permission of BOA Editions, Ltd., 260 East Avenue, Rochester, NY 14604.

Elizabeth Coatsworth: "And Stands There Sighing" reprinted with permission from *The Christian Science Monitor*. Copyright © 1956 by The Christian Science Publishing Society. All rights reserved. "This Is a Night" reprinted with the permission of Simon & Schuster Books for Young Readers, an imprint of Simon & Schuster Children's Publishing Division from *Down Half the World* by Elizabeth Coatsworth. Copyright © 1968 by Elizabeth Coatsworth Beston.

Frances Conford: "Childhood" from *Collected Poems* by Frances Conford. Published by Cresset Press. Reproduced by permission of Hutchinson.

E. E. Cummings: "in Just-" copyright 1923, 1951 © 1991 by the Trustees for the E. E. Cummings Trust. Copyright © 1976 by George James Firmage, from *Complete Poems: 1904–1962* by E. E. Cummings. Edited by George J. Firmage. Reprinted by permission of Liveright Publishing Corporation.

Walter de la Mare: "The Old Stone House" from *Peacock Pie: A Book of Rhymes*. Reprinted by permission of the Literary Trustees of Walter de la Mare, and the